# Shall we have another

MOSAICA PRESS

# Shall we have another

## A JEWISH APPROACH TO FAMILY PLANNING

### MENDEL DUBOV

Published by Mosaica Press, Inc.
www.mosaicapress.com
info@mosaicapress.com

## אברהם אזדאבא
חבר הבד"צ דק"ק קראון הייטס

# Rabbi Avrohom Osdoba
602 Montgomery Street
Brooklyn, New York 11225
(718) 771-8737

ב"ה

יום א' לפ' 'והי' זרעך כעפר הארץ', ג' כסלו ה'תשע"ט

לכבוד נכדי היקר הרב מ"מ שיחי' דובאוו - ת"ח מובהק בקי בהלכות שונות ובפרט בהלכות יום-יומיים, עוסק בעבודת הקודש לקרב הרחוקים לשמירת התורה והמצוה.

ראיתי ספר החשוב שמצא חן בעיני ע"ד המשך הולדת בנים ובנות בישראל. ספר כזה מועיל לבאר בטוב טעם השקפת תורתנו הק' בנידון והמסתעף, כל זה כפי שהוא מואר בתורת חסידות חב"ד ושיחות רבותינו נשיאנו זי"ע.

ספר זה נחוץ מאד ובפרט בזמן הזה אפילו לשומר תורה ומצוות שלא יהא נמשך אחר השקפות העולם שמחלזלים במצוה חשובה כזה "מצות פרו ורבו" - מצוה הראשונה בתורתנו הקדושה.

מובטחני שבעז"ה יהי' ספר זה לתועלת ולעידוד בני ובנות ישראל שי' בקבלת ברכת ה' בהולדת עוד בנים ובנות בשמחה ובטוב לבב, כדברי חז"ל "א"ר יהושע הי' לו בנים בילדותו יהיו לו בנים בזקנתו וכו'" (יבמות סב, ב).

ע"ז באתי על החתום בברכה להצלחה רבה, ושנזכה לגאולה האמיתית והשלימה שכדרז"ל "אין בן דוד בא עד שיכלו כל הנשמות שבגוף" (ע"ז ה, א).

שלום דוד שלאם בלא"ה

חתימה

Rabbi Hershel Schachter
24 Bennett Avenue
New York, New York 10033
(212) 795-0630

הרב צבי שכטר
ראש ישיבה ורם כולל
ישיבת רבינו יצחק אלחנן

מזכה דרבים

בע"ה נעבר המונרת שנו ה

...

בברכת התורה

אליעזר שכטר

**Rabbi G. Zinner**

*of Cong. Nitei Gavriel*

1541 40th Street,

Brooklyn, NY 11218

גבריאל צינער

רב דק"ק ומח"ס

נטעי גבריאל

ברוקלין, ניו יארק

ר"ח סיון מ"ה למב"י תשע"ט לפ"ק

בס"ד

הנה הרה"ח, אוצר בלום של תורה ויר"ש, מוכתר בנימוסין, נועם
הליכות והמדות, עוסק בהרבצת תורה וחסידות לרבים, איש האשכולות,
הרב **מנחם מענדל דובאוו** שליט"א, הראה לי פרי עטו בו הוא מלקט
כעומר גורנה, ומבאר ומעורר את הרבים גודל החיוב של מצוה הראשונה
פו"ר, וכדרשת חז"ל עה"פ בבקר זרע זרעך ולערב אל תנח ידך. והוא מביא
ברכה וטובה לעולם. וידוע כמה התריע כ"ק אדמו"ר מליובאוויטש זי"ע
ע"ז, ובפרט אחר המלחמה הנוראה שרבבות מאלפי ישראל קדושים
וטהורים עלו על המוקדה עקדה"ש, שחובה על אחד למלאות החסרון.

לכן אמינא לפעלא טבא יישר כחו וחילו לאורייתא, וחפץ ה' בידו
יצליח להרבות חיילים לתורה, ובודאי יתקבלו דבריו ויעשו אות
לטובה, ובזכות זה נזכה לביאת דוד מלכא משיחא, וכמאחז"ל אין בן
דוד בא עד שיכלו כל הנשמות שבגוף, והזמן גרמא כדאיתא בזוה"ק בחג
השבועות יפקון בני ישראל מן גלותא, בב"א.

החותם בברכה

נ"ב
מובן ופשוט שבדברים אלו כ"א יהא לו רב ומורה דרך, אשר על פיו ישק כל דבר.

**Rabbi Gedalia Oberlander**
CONG. HEICHAL MENACHEM of MONSEY

גדלי' אבערלאנדער
רב דקהל היכל מנחם – מאנסי

עורך קובץ אור ישראל ס"ח היכל הבעש"ט ומח"ס פדיון הבן כהלכתו, בתיבות התפילה, מנהג אבותינו בידינו, נרות שבת כהלכה, כללי טהרה
51 Park Lane, Monsey, NY 10952 Phone/Fax 845-426-7321

ב"ה

יום כ"ח לחודש הגאולה ניסן תשע"ט

### הסכמה

בואו ונחזיק טובה להאי גברא יקירא חיכו ממתקים וכולו מחמדים, כ"ש הרה"ת מוה"ר מנחם מענדל דוביאו שליט"א, אשר הובא לפני חלק מספרו על השקפת התורה והגישה היהודית לתכנון משפחה וגידול הברכה בהולדת ילדים, והכל בלשון צח וברור השוה לכל נפש ובשפת המדינה.

ודבר גדול עשה בעמיו שהרי מצוה ראשונה בתורה היא מצות פרו ורבו והיא אמורה בלשון של ברכה שכן אין ברכה גדולה ליחיד ולכלל כברכת הפריון והריבוי, ולא היו צריכים לכתוב בדבר הפשוט כל כך ומובן מאליו אלמלא רוחות חדשות וזרות שחדרו אל כרם בית ישראל רוחות של תכנון משפחה, וכבר ידועים הדברים המובאים בשם השל"ה הק' שהקב"ה צוה בתורה פרו ורבו מובן שעם כל ילד נוסף שנולד נפתח צינור חדש ומשפיע פרנסה גם לילד הנוסף שזה עתה נולד, כמו כן מעניק הקב"ה להורים את הכוחות הנצרכים להם לגדל את הילד.

ובנוסף לברכה הפרטית לההורים בילד נוסף הרי זה גם מקרבת את הגאולה לכללות ישראל כמבואר בגמ' (יבמות סב, ב) אין בן דוד בא עד שיכלו כל הנשמות שבגוף, ועלינו לעשות את התלוי בנו כדי למהר את הגאולה השלימה.

ויהי רצון שיזכה לברך על המוגמר להדפיס הספר, ויפוצו ביעקב ויחלקו בישראל, ויתקבלו דבריו בין המוני בית ישראל הרוצים בברכת ה'.

והנני בא בברכה להרב המחבר שליט"א שבזכות זיכוי הרבים יצליח בכל אשר יפנה, ויפוצו מעיינותיו חוצה.

המברך בברכת התורה ללומדיה בלו"נ.

דוד ני אבערלאנדער

בס"ד

**R' Chaim Mayer Roth**
**Rav Sterling Forest Sfard**
**1 White Dove**
**Lakewood N.J.**

חיים מאיר ראטה
רב דשטערלינג פארעסט ספרד
ליקוואוד יצ"ו
732-961-7791

**מכתב ברכה**

לכבוד הרב מנחם מנדל דובאוו שליט"א,

קיבלתי הכתבים שלך הנכתבים בשפת המדינה, וגם דיברתי אתך בטלפון, ונהנתי מאד שהכנסת עצמך לתוך נושא גדול הלזה. וכפי שידוע לכל מי שעוסק עם הציבור היהודית הרחב בזמן הזה, נושא זה צריך חיזוק גדול. כי האוירה של חיים נוחים מצד אחד, וגודל עול הפרנסה שחופפת על כל משפחה מצד השני, הם משפיעים מאד על רוחם ודעתם של בני אדם. ולכן בודאי דבר טוב קבלת על עצמך לחזק לעם ה' עם השקפה הנכונה על פי תורה, כדי שיהי' להם לתריס נגד הרוחות החזקות שהם נושבות, שהוא נעשה כמו חומה לעמוד נגדם. ולא עוד אלא שבודאי גם לאותם שאין להם נסיון בענין זה, כדאי להם לדעת האמת מה הוא האושר הגדול מקיום של מצוה זו, שידעו כי הוא מן הדברים החשובים ביותר, שהרי הוא קיום העולם כלו, והנצחיות של עם ישראל.

היות ואין מדרכי להיות מן המסכימים, ובודאי לא בנושא רגיש שהוא עדין ביותר, ולכן קשה עלי ליתן הסכמה, אבל ראיתי שקיבלת הסכמות מרבנים ופוסקים אחרים, ואין צורך לדידי וכווותי. אבל בודאי ברכתי אליך שהקב"ה תברך אותך עם סייעתא דשמיא לעורר עם ה' עם דבר ה' בחיזוק הראוי על פי תורה כרצונך הטוב. ויה"ר שתתברך עם הברכה שכתב התורה לשפרה ופועה שעשו במסירת נפש עבור קיום הנצחי של כלל ישראל, "וייטב אלקים למילדות וירב העם ויעצמו מאד", שכתבו כמה מפרשים שהברכה שהברכה הכי גדולה והטבה הכי גדולה שהי' יכול הקב"ה לברך אותם הוא שיצליחו במעשיהם להיות העם מתרבה על ידם, ויה"ר שגם מע"כ תברך בברכה זו ותצליח מעשה ידיך שתצא מזה התעוררות גדול לעם ישראל וירב העם ויעצמו מאד.

מתוך הערצה וברכה,

חיים מאיר ראטה

*Letter of Blessing*

B"H

It gives us great delight to share our eager approbation to the work of our dear son Rabbi Mendel Dubov, entitled *Shall We Have Another? A Jewish Approach To Family Planning.*

Throughout history, our people have faced both internal and external challenges. In today's day and age, the Torah value of having a large family has become a subject of intense discussion in the Jewish community. For Jewish couples today, few conversations rival the importance and necessity of this one.

We are certain that this wonderful book will enhance the ability of any reader to properly articulate the timeless truths of Torah as they pertain to this particular subject. Chazal state that the coming of Mashiach is dependent on all souls descending into a body. May it be the will of Hashem that this book bring about the birth of those final souls that will precipitate the Geulah speedily in our days.

It is a source of great *nachas* to us that Mendel has written this valuable and timely work, with the support of his *eishes chayil* Chava Mushkah and the wonderful kids. May Hashem bless them all in good health and with all blessings both materially and spiritually.

With our blessings,

Rabbi and Mrs. Nissan Dovid and Sarah Dubov

# *Table of Contents*

## PART 1
## *Shall We Have Another?*

# *Preface*

THE IDEA for this book came from a deeply personal place. Both my wife and I come from large families. Soon after we were married, we were blessed with our first child. Our second did not take long to follow. Within a short few years, our home was filled with, thank G-d, many healthy and lively children.

Raising happy, competent, and socially adept children is no small task for parents. This is magnified manifold when a couple chooses to have a large family. The resources of strength, time, money, and stamina that are necessary for such an endeavor are huge. Doing justice to having many children means that the lives of their parents must revolve around them. Putting other interests above raising one's children will inevitably be putting them at a disadvantage.

Following our parents' examples and with reflection on our own, my wife and I both felt fortunate to count ourselves among the many families who happily fulfilled the injunction to "be fruitful and multiply." But, as with everything that is both important and demanding, we often felt the need for motivation and inspiration.

This would be true of any issue and at any time and age. What places this subject in a different category than many others is the fact that, in our time, having a large family has become difficult both inside and outside the home. Common culture and practice have gone in the very opposite direction of a pronatalist approach. Today, having large families is often seen as selfish, or even a bad idea. One of the hardest things in human nature is to go against the cultural current. History and modern-day statistics are the strongest portrayers of this reality.

The need for a comprehensive and thorough compilation of a Jewish viewpoint on the subject has never been greater.

The research and writing of this work have been rewarding and inspiring. While the Jewish sources on the subject are found throughout classical Judaism, this book is in large measure based upon the teachings of Chabad and the many talks of the Lubavitcher Rebbe, Rabbi Menachem M. Schneerson, of blessed memory.

The reader is urged to note that this book comes to address the general Jewish perspective on this subject. In this sense, it is not a book of Jewish law, but rather an examination of its spirit.

The subject of this work speaks to some of the most crucial decisions a married couple will ever make. It is my hope and prayer to G-d that I successfully convey the voice of our sacred tradition in this vital conversation.

# Acknowledgments

I WISH to thank the many rabbis and teachers who gave me their encouragement and guidance throughout this project. A special thanks to Mrs. Miriam Chana Miller for her initial edit of the work.

My great appreciation goes out to Rabbi Yaacov Haber, Rabbi Doron Kornbluth, and the dedicated team at Mosaica Press for bringing this project to the finish line.

Finally, to my dear parents, siblings, and extended family for their endless love and support.

To all our beloved children with whom we have been so incredibly blessed.

And to my wife חוה מושקא ת׳. "The feeling of the heart cannot be put into writing." This book, and so much more, would be completely impossible without her.

הודו לה׳ כי טוב כי לעולם חסדו

Mendel Dubov

Kislev 5779 / 2018

Sparta, NJ

XV

# Introduction

## PLANNING FOR LESS

Limiting the number of children per family has universally been accepted as a given in the modern world—and not in moderation.

Consider a simple comparison: Around the year 1800, the average woman in the US had seven or eight children.[1] At the time of writing, the average fertility rate per woman in the US is 1.76,[2] and in Europe, 1.55.[3] Similar rates are reflected in most developed countries.

This phenomenon has many contributing factors. An obvious one is the open market of effective, simple-to-use, and cheap methods of birth control. More important, however, is what has fueled the market of the various birth control methods: the massive change of societal attitude regarding this issue.

Over the last two centuries, the modern birth control movement has changed the lives of women and men, regardless of race, culture, or

1    "Family Life: Courtship and Marriage," *American Eras*, 1997, Encyclopedia.com, 22 Nov. 2015.

2    https://data.worldbank.org/indicator/SP.DYN.TFRT.IN?locations=US&name_desc=false.

3    http://ec.europa.eu/eurostat/statistics-explained/index.php/Fertility_statistics.

religion. Given the choice, most couples in developed countries decide to severely limit the number of children they have. Why?

Let us look at some of the most common explanations.

## Difficulty for Parents

Raising a child, with the kind of devotion he or she deserves, involves tremendous sacrifice on the part of the parents in any number of the following areas:

- Financial strain: The breadwinner(s) of the household must provide for and educate children until they are self-sufficient. Often, the financial status of the family is such that the family cannot afford another child if the current standard of living is to be maintained. An additional child means either compromising on this standard or having to work harder (and more).
- Physical and emotional strain: Raising children in the proper manner demands a huge amount of bodily strength and emotional stamina. In addition, fewer pregnancies and births is an obvious ease on a woman's health.
- Inconvenience: The endless chores and responsibilities that increase with every child are a great deterrent to having more children. On a broader level, parents find it difficult or even impossible to fulfill some (often, even many) of their own desires and aspirations while caring for their families. Having another child could mean a major delay or cancellation of a career or project (especially for mothers), an inability to participate in various social affairs, difficulty in traveling long distances, and so on.
- Fear and anxiety: A child lives in the hearts of their parents constantly. Parents worry for the health and well-being of their children even after the child is an adult and is no longer dependent on them. This is true even more so for parents of young children. This constant concern exists even if everything is going well for the child, and all the more so if they are more challenged. More children seem to multiply parental anxiety.

## Disadvantages for Children

Often, it is the well-being of the children themselves that creates a strong argument for having fewer of them: Can parents possibly devote themselves properly to a large number of children? It seems obvious that the fewer the children, the more attention and devotion the parents can provide. The economic factor plays a large role here as well; with most families living on a limited budget, the larger the family, the fewer the opportunities that can be offered to each child.

## Environmental Concerns

Having fewer children has become very popular in many spheres of public influence. Concerns of overpopulating the planet have given room for some strong arguments in favor of limiting the number of humans living on it. In many parts of the world, cutting down the number of children seems to be the only answer in an economy that already finds it difficult to sustain its current population. From such perspectives, small families constitute a wise—and even moral—lifestyle.

## Social Acceptance

In most developed countries there is a stigma attached to large families. They are regarded as primitive at best, and irresponsible or even reckless at worst. Parents of large families are often confronted with an entire gamut of attitudes and comments, some of which can be quite difficult and hurtful. Often, modern society is not accepting of children altogether, let alone many of them.

For some, there are other considerations that at least contribute to the decision of having fewer children.

- Lack of parental efficacy: Many couples—or one of the spouses—do not see themselves as the ideal parents. They feel incompetent in performing the various tasks that are the basics of parenthood. Included may be those who naturally find it altogether difficult relating to and working with young people and children.

- Cosmetic concerns: To many, the deleterious effect of pregnancy and childbirth to the beauty of the woman is a cause for limiting childbearing to a minimum. Aside from her own self-image, the cosmetic concern may extend to the workplace or to the marital relationship with her husband.

## SELFISH OR ALTRUISTIC?

Trends in modern lifestyles can either be good, bad, or a mixture of both. Of course, not everything popular is always noble or even moral. In this case, however, the normative social behavior seems to be logically compelling, even moral and altruistic, not to mention allowing for a much calmer and more convenient lifestyle.

Perhaps even more fascinating is that the underlying motives for the arguments presented above (the "fewer kids is better" approach) would seem to be quite concurrent with Jewish values:

- Financial strain: Torah sources abound with the idea that we should not be excessively involved in material matters, for this distracts from spiritual pursuits.[4] A large family, in most cases, involves the investment of much more time and energy in order to provide and care for them than a smaller family does.
- Physical, mental, and emotional strain: It is a Torah instruction to care for our health and well-being and not to cause any unnecessary risk or strain to our bodies.[5] Large families are more strenuous.
- Convenience: Although the Torah does not encourage the pursuit of material pleasures for their own sake, the Torah endlessly encourages us to fill our lives with Torah study and mitzvah fulfillment. Having a large family could surely inhibit the ability to devote oneself to many other worthy causes.
- Disadvantage to the children: This too comes across as a rather compelling Torah argument. When doing a mitzvah—and

---

4    See *Rambam, Hilchos Talmud Torah* 3:6-9; *Shulchan Aruch, Orach Chaim* 156.
5    See *Rambam, Hilchos Deos* 4:1; *Rema, Yoreh Deah* 116:5.

childbearing is a mitzvah—we are enjoined to do it in the best way we can. Regarding the supplicatory additions to prayer, we are told, "Better a little said with proper concentration than a lot with no concentration."[6] Having many children seems to compromise the quality of education and upbringing in relationship to the quantity of children.

- Lack of parental efficacy: The Torah teaches that not everyone is expected to excel in the same spiritual area as another.[7] For example, some do better in the learning and teaching of Torah, and some are better in the world of charity and good deeds.[8] While every Jew must fulfill all the mitzvos, not everyone can excel in everything. What if someone is not naturally a great parent—should they really have a large family?

- Environmental concerns: The Torah has an environmental ethic which is central to Jewish law and life. Damage to the environment or natural resources is an obvious Torah concern.[9]

- Cosmetic concerns: The Torah is highly sensitive to the necessity of beauty to a woman, and often makes concessions in the law to uphold this.[10]

- Spiritual concerns: To the Jew, an added dimension to the above is the concern for the spiritual well-being of the children. The challenges in educating children are many and great. Constantly lingering in the hearts of devoted Jewish parents is the concern of whether they will be fully successful in raising their child in a Torah way. With large families, can parents really give the time, money, focus, and attention necessary to ensure their children have a love and respect for the Torah values that they hold dear?

Yet, despite these considerations, the position of Torah is unequivocal: *Children are a blessing.* As a rule, Jewish couples should always

---

6    *Shulchan Aruch, Orach Chaim* 1:4.

7    See *Shabbos* 118B.

8    See *Bereishis Rabbah* 99:8.

9    See *Rambam, Hilchos Melachim* 6:10.

10   See *Kesubos* 59b; *Shulchan Aruch, Orach Chaim* 103:18 and 613:10; *Yoreh Deah* 381:6.

endeavor to have an additional child, should the opportunity arise. The sources will be elaborated upon throughout this book, but the bottom line is clear and unanimous.

Inevitably, according to the Torah, bringing another child into the world overrides all the considerations listed above:

Having another Jewish child is worth all the difficulty and distraction surrounding it, whether it be physical and emotional strain, or the consumption of time and effort meeting financial needs. The time and energy necessary for more Torah study and mitzvah performance are secondary to caring for and raising another child. While quality and efficacy are obviously important, concern for these should not have any bearing on the size of a Jewish family. Care must be taken for the environment we live in, and the maintenance of a woman's beauty is important, but the imperative of having another Jewish child is supreme.

To be sure, there are exceptions to the application of this principal. Sometimes, certain considerations do take priority.[11] This, however, is the *exception*. As a rule, the principled Jewish view encouraging the birth of another child is clear.

## A MODERN ISSUE

"Modernity is the transition from fate to choice."[12]

The modern age has brought with it radical challenges to accepted norms. One notable expression of this has been the limitation of family size. The mere fact that large families were considered a good idea in the past does not evidently motivate the modern generation to follow suit. After all, unlike the pursuit of material comfort, the act of having many children does not seem to offer the average modern couple any

---

11   See part 4.
12   *The Dignity of Difference*, Rabbi Lord Jonathan Sacks (Bloomsbury Academic; 2003) p. 109.

kind of gratification. The majority, it seems, see having a large family as a sacrifice they are unwilling to make.

Insofar as the Jewish people are concerned, the difficulty in accepting the Torah stance on this subject is not a new phenomenon.[13] The challenge has only been magnified with the advent of modern-day family planning standards. Moreover, it is important to understand that the Jewish approach presents a challenge even to the Jew who is accustomed to viewing and living life according to Torah. Rabbis, mentors, and educators can attest to the fact that this area is one of the most challenging in Jewish life today.

When it comes to many of life's questions, we are accustomed to having the ability to delve into the texts and Rabbinic responsa of our long history. This remains vital, of course; however, in this area, things have radically changed, and many new questions and possibilities have arisen. Many factors have come together and created a situation that was inconceivable even just a century ago:

- On the one hand, advances of medical science and fertility treatment have made it possible for many more couples to have children, and to have them at lower risk.

- On the other hand, the ease and safety of curtailing childbirth while maintaining a regular married life have never been greater.

---

13    An example can be found in the writings of Rav Chaim Ben Attar (1696–1743) in his commentary *Ohr Hachaim* on the Torah. He bemoans the conduct of "some members of our people" who after having enough children to "continue the species" will no longer endeavor to bring any more children into the world (*Bereishis* 1:28). See also *Sefer Hachaim* (Rav Chaim Ben Betzalel, brother of the Maharal of Prague, circ. 1530–1588); *Sefer Chaim Tovim*, chap. 1; *Pele Yoetz* (Rav Eliezer Papu, 1786–1827) entry for *Priyah Verivyah*.

Conversely, see *Emunos V'Deos* (Rav Saadia Gaon, 882–942), essay 9, chap. 10. In his time and place, there seemed to have been an obsession by some to beget as many children as possible. *Emunos V'Deos* criticizes such conduct, for most of the explanations cited above: financial strain, the lack of sufficient educational attention, strain and danger to the mother's health, parental anxiety, the high demands for keeping the children's health, and the insecurity of the children's physical and spiritual future. He concludes that "the correct way in it is, with [the number of] children which G-d will favor his servant as He desires... it is dear to a person that he should hold by that which G-d has favored him, and not overly rouse on this matter." (See however *Pele Yoetz*, ibid., who encourages the investment of medical and conjugal effort in order to have additional children.)

- On top of all this, the modern era has brought massive social change as to the role of the woman, along with the overwhelming prevalence and acceptance of limiting family size.

For most of our history, having a large family was actually far from simple. The following description gives us an idea of what reality might have looked like for a Jewish family in ancient times:

> *Inadequate nutrition and the presence of endemic and epidemic disease to which children are especially susceptible a priori suggest that infant mortality was high... Ancient Greece probably had an infant mortality rate of fifty to seventy percent, figures similar to the fifty to sixty percent mortality rate in medieval Italy. Other mortality tables, without including the effects of endemic disease, suggest about fifty percent for the first five years of life...As high as these figures are, they do not take into account lost fetuses resulting from miscarriages (which today can terminate as many as thirty percent of pregnancies), preterm stillborns, and other complications of pregnancy. Consequently, with a survival rate of about fifty percent, having three children surviving beyond the age of five would have entailed as many as six pregnancies—or more, if preterm losses are included.[14]*

The above is just one dimension of how, thankfully, we can in no way compare family life today to that of our ancestors. Thus, it is not surprising that little of our pre-modern literature addresses this issue in the way we perceive it today.

The Jewish perspective on dealing with the question at hand reflects the same attitude we are to have to all other modern Jewish questions and challenges: we are to look back into the Torah for direction. The Torah, which is Divine and eternal, will never fail to provide answers and guidance to any subject that affects our purpose here on earth, despite new technologies and attitudes. This subject is no exception.

---

14   Carol Meyers, *Rediscovering Eve: Ancient Israelite Women in Context* (Oxford University Press, New York, 2012), p. 98.

As Jews, we can ill afford to neglect adequately addressing this issue. Human nature dictates that, as a rule, we fall back on the social standards of the world around us. It is never easy to be different, let alone when there is such a high cost attached to it.

"Shall we have another?" is a question that, thankfully, most Jewish couples are able to consider at various points in their lives. The prevailing attitudes range from one extreme to another:

- For many, after having the number of children they planned for (or more), the prospect of having another will be met by a conclusive decision in the negative.
- On the other extreme, many Jewish parents will not entertain the question at all. Providing it is medically safe, their decision is to have as many children as the Almighty will grant them.

The middle ground to the above will be the thoughtful and serious consideration by many couples whether to have an additional child.

Importantly, the above middle ground will also contain the question of "spacing." As opposed to a "yes or no" scenario, many couples will at some point ask themselves, "Shall we have another *now*?"

Many Jewish couples are at least basically aware of the Torah's approach to this subject. It is no secret, however, that in this area we are witness to an unfortunate state of affairs in many Jewish families:

- Total resignation. The knowledge of the Torah perspective is so rudimentary and feeble that it fails to stand up to the pervasive culture and desire for an easier way of life. "I really admire those who do this but...no. Not me."
- Partial resignation. Often, the actual deed is fulfilled not out of inner conviction, but due to a social norm of family and friends, coupled with the knowledge that this is "the right thing to do." The trouble with such an approach is that it is constantly put to test. The obligations taken with having a large family are immense. Sadly, what often follows is also a kind of resignation—maybe not from having more children—but from the full devotion of caring and properly raising them.
- A minimalist approach. This will be the examination of the exact religious obligation, with a strong leaning toward the more

lenient authorities in the field, thus minimizing any excessive invasion to a current view of life.

The following chapters will explore the Jewish approach to this highly important and sensitive subject. Naturally, there are few who enter this conversation with no previous thoughts or notions. In this vein, the appeal goes out to the reader to come with an open mind and, to those whom these chapters directly affect, an open heart. This book is not the end of the conversation, but rather the beginning.

As mentioned earlier, our discussion here comes to explain the Jewish approach to this issue and to put this delicate question into its proper context. It is important to emphasize, however, that final decisions in this matter are highly particular to the circumstances of each individual family. As such, it is vital for a couple to be properly aware of their situation and to be in ongoing contact with a qualified rabbi who can provide specialized guidance in this matter.

Having said this, the *sine qua non*—the crucial element in all the above—is putting the question in context. As such, the material in this work is relevant to everyone.

# Shall We Have Another?

*While conducting an interview with a particularly large Jewish family, a news reporter asked the father to comment on what brought him and his wife to have so many children. In response, the father had all the children sit around the dining room table. "Now," said the father, "would you kindly point out which child here is extra?"*

# CHAPTER 1

# *Law—and Spirit*

BEFORE RECEIVING the Torah at Mount Sinai, the Jewish people affirmed their acceptance of the Divine gift with the words "*naaseh v'nishma*—we will do and then seek to understand."[1] The indication here is that the bond of a Jew to G-d and His Torah is an essential and total one, and, as such, not relegated to the limitations of understanding. Even if he cannot relate to it intellectually, a Jew will follow the Torah with happiness and contentment, knowing that there can be nothing better than abiding by the Divine manual for life.

On the other hand, this very same statement also indicates the necessity of "*nishma*," the understanding. The Torah and its precepts must become part of who we are, both intellectually and emotionally. Insofar as our subject is concerned, the *nishma* element has become increasingly critical.

Most commandments in the Torah are quite specific. Observing Shabbos, laying tefillin, consuming kosher food, following the laws of family purity—these mitzvos and many others all have a defined character. In any given situation, we can readily determine whether the mitzvah is being observed or not. But then there are mitzvos that

---

1   *Shemos* 24:7 as explained in *Shabbos* 88a.

are not merely about a specific action. The practical applications of these mitzvos are rather an expression of a fundamental idea, an idea that, at times, may not be evident from the technical application of the mitzvah.

An example for this can be found in the mitzvah of Torah study. In Jewish life, the study of Torah is endlessly extolled and emphasized. As we state each day in our prayers, "For this [Torah] is our life and the length of our days." The Torah is our connection to G-d, without which we are, in the famous words of Rabbi Akiva, like fish without water.[2]

The above finds expression in the fact that for a Jew, learning Torah can never end. "You shall speak of them when you sit in your house and when you walk on the road, when you lie down, and when you rise."[3] The joy and pleasure of the Jew should always be found in the study of Torah. The fact that a person may fulfill the obligation of Torah study with set times for doing so is only in view of the fact that he may have other responsibilities that take precedence over Torah study.

In one instance, our Sages expressed this in a fascinating way. When speaking of the obligation of an otherwise busy person to study Torah, the Talmudic and halachic term is *"kevius itim l'Torah*—establishing fixed times for Torah." The Talmud famously states that when a person passes from this world, one of the first questions he is asked is, "Did you establish fixed times for Torah study?"[4]

What is quite surprising is that on other occasions, our Sages express extreme disfavor for this very idea: "One who establishes fixed times to study Torah has forsaken the Torah" or "has forsaken the covenant"![5]

How can the Sages both recommend and disapprove of fixed times for Torah study?

One of the explanations given is that the later statements refer to a person who keeps precisely to his fixed times for study and never studies outside of them. Such a person sees Torah study as a chore, or worse

---

2   See *Berachos* 61b.
3   *Devarim* 6:7.
4   *Shabbos* 31a.
5   See *Yalkut Tehillim* 119 (R. 878); *Yerushalmi Berachos*, chap. 9.

still, as a burden. Thus, although he may have technically fulfilled his obligation, the entire concept has been lost on him.[6]

Another example can be found in the mitzvah of tzedakah (charity). Here again, the Torah endlessly extols the greatness of this mitzvah. Tzedakah is the hallmark of the Jewish people, as the Torah states regarding Avraham, "I [G-d] have known him, because he commands his children...to perform charity."[7] "Charity is equivalent to all the other mitzvos combined," states the Talmud.[8] As far as the law goes, "we are obligated to be careful with regard to the mitzvah of charity to a greater extent than all other positive commandments."[9] In all of the *Talmud Yerushalmi*, charity is simply known as "the mitzvah." The expression of this value can be found in the endless and boundless devotion to charitable endeavors by Jews throughout the ages.

Now, in Jewish law there are specifications of how much, when, and to whom tzedakah should be distributed.[10] It is obvious, however, that these are technical parameters to an idea that is essentially boundless. The legal limitations on tzedakah are only there to ensure that it does not detract from a person's other responsibilities (as well as ensuring the integrity of the receiver). In many instances, these limitations are to be ignored if a time or situation of necessity arises.[11] At times like these, our Sages strongly warn against keeping to the regulated form of charity.[12] Any attempt, therefore, to define the *concept* of tzedakah by its *regulations* is flawed.

Other examples of this nature exist in the negative arena: Marriage between a Jew and a non-Jew is widely known as one of the greatest tragedies that can befall a Jewish person. What is interesting is that the Torah does not include intermarriage in the same category as most of the other forbidden relationships. Legally speaking, most of the other forbidden

---

6   *Birkei Yosef, Machzik Berachah, siman* 156; *Kuntres Etz Hachaim*, chap. 26.

7   *Bereishis* 18:19.

8   *Bava Basra* 9a.

9   *Rambam, Hilchos Matnos Aniyim* 10:1.

10   See *Shulchan Aruch, Yoreh Deah, simanim* 249–51.

11   See *Igeres Hakodesh* 10; *Shaarei Tzedakah (Kehot)*, p. 167 ff.

12   See, for example, *Igeres Hakodesh* 16.

relationships are considered a cardinal sin, biblically punishable by death, whereas a relationship with a non-Jew is not treated as such.

This fact, however, cannot at all be seen as a diminishing factor to the gravity of the concept. Even when the parties do not marry, the very nature of such a relationship is a betrayal of one's entire Jewish identity: "This matter causes one to cling to the gentile nations from whom the Holy One Blessed Be He has separated us, and to turn away from following G-d and to betray Him."[13] In other words, the *legal* consequences of intermarriage, serious as they are, do not in any way portray its true meaning and ramifications.

In summary, the intensity of a mitzvah may not be evident from its legal aspects, and it can often only be found in wider Torah sources. "The words of Torah may be 'poor' in one place but 'rich' in another," say our Sages.[14]

All the above will allow for a proper understanding of the topic at hand.

The Torah instructs us to have children: "Be fruitful and multiply."[15] As will be elaborated upon at length, the Torah sees infinite importance and blessing in every additional Jewish life here on earth. This is such a basic and fundamental idea that, as will be demonstrated, the Torah tells this to us in many places as a matter of fact. Towing the line of the Torah, the Sages instructed that a couple not end their procreation at a minimum but rather continue having more children, if possible.[16]

Now, similar to the many examples cited above, here too there is a technical minimum of how many children a person must have in order

---

13  *Rambam, Hilchos Issurei Biah* 12:8.

14  *Yerushalmi Rosh Hashanah* 17a.

15  It is interesting to note that, as pertaining to mankind, this injunction actually appears twice. The first is directed to Adam and Chavah (*Bereishis* 1:28), the second to Noach after the flood (ibid., 9:7). Most authorities understand the first to be an empowerment and a blessing, and only the second to be a commandment. *Sefer Hachinuch*, however, chooses to elaborate on the commandment of having children using the verse pertaining to Adam and Chavah. The Mishnah (*Yevamos* 6:6) also quotes the verse pertaining to Adam and Chavah as the source of the opinion that both men and women are obligated in procreation.

16  *Talmud Yevamos* 62b; *Rambam, Hilchos Ishus* 15:16.

to fulfill the Biblical mitzvah.[17] Following this, there is much halachic discussion as to the exact criteria and character of the Rabbinical mitzvah of continuing to procreate.[18] One thing is certain, however: before any discussion regarding this mitzvah can commence, we must first have a real understanding of its underlying concepts.

Why is having another child so important?

Let us begin.

---

17 See *Mishnah Yevamos* 6:6; *Tosefta Yevamos* 8; *Shulchan Aruch, Even Ha'ezer* 1:5–6. See at length *Otzar Haposkim*, ad loc.

18 *Ramban Baal Hamaor* to *Talmud Yevamos* ibid; *Sdei Chemed*, vol. 5, p.141; *Aruch Hashulchan Even Ha'ezer* 1:8; *Likutei Sichos*, vol. 30, p. 24 ff. (For further sources and analysis, see article by R.A. Alinson, *Noam,* vol. 19, p. 256.)

# CHAPTER 2

# *An Approach*

## FIRST AND FOREMOST

The word Torah stems from the Hebrew word *"hora'ah*—teaching." The objective of Torah is to teach man how to live. Aside for the instruction in the actual text, the Torah uses multiple methods, often subtle, in conveying its instructions for life.

One of the above methods is that of textual order. The accounts in the Torah do not answer to natural or chronological sequence, and there is intended precision to the order in which the various passages appear.[1]

Our Sages make the observation that the very first instruction recorded in the Torah is to "be fruitful and multiply."[2] Now, when it comes to the Ten Commandments, the first mitzvah is that of knowing G-d—"I am the L-rd thy G-d." The rationale for this is obvious. To use the words of our Sages, it is first necessary to "accept G-d's sovereignty

---

1    See *Pesachim* 6b.

2    As has been noted earlier, this injunction as it was given to Adam and Chavah is, according to many, more of a blessing than a commandment. Following this approach, the actual commandment was first given to Noach. Regardless of whether this passage is considered a blessing or an actual command, the phrase definitely contains an instruction.

and then to accept His decrees."[3] We follow this pattern in the daily reading of the *Shema* where we preface the first paragraph, which speaks of G-d's Oneness, to the second, which speaks of the observance of the commandments. Once again, the reason given is because "one should first accept upon oneself the yoke of Heaven and after this the yoke of the mitzvos."[4]

Nevertheless, it was this commandment, over all others, that was chosen to appear first in the Torah. Simply speaking, it can be basically understood using the observation of *Sefer Hachinuch*: "This is a great mitzvah, for through it, all the other mitzvos in the Torah may be fulfilled; for the mitzvos were given to man, and not to the ministering angels."[5] In other words, the prerequisite to all other commandments is the presence of man to whom the command is being directed.

On a deeper level, a Chassidic interpretation explains it in the following way:

Childbirth appears as the first instruction in the Torah because, on a certain level, the function of the entire Torah is to bring out the greatness of the Jewish people. This was expressed by the Sage Hillel in his famous statement regarding the mitzvah of loving one's fellow: "This is the entire Torah; the rest is commentary."[6] As such, the Torah begins with the mitzvah of procreation because, first and foremost, "A Jew must desire the existence of another Jew."[7]

This "desire for another Jew" is actually reflected in the terminology that the Torah uses in the instruction, "Be fruitful and multiply." Why the double expression? *Rashi* explains: "If [the verse] had only said, 'be fruitful,' one would beget one and no more; 'and multiply' was therefore said so that one could beget many."[8]

This is the first example of the priority the Torah gives to childbirth, and the immediate emphasis on the intent to have "many." This idea

---

3    See *Rashi* to *Vayikra* 18:2.

4    *Mishnah Berachos* 2:1.

5    *Sefer Hachinuch*, mitzvah 1.

6    *Shabbos* 31a; See *Maharsha* ad loc.

7    *Sefer Hasichos* 5696, p. 119. See also *Likutei Dibburim*, vol. 4, p. 746.

8    *Bereishis* 1:22, where the terms are used for the first time regarding marine life and birds.

continues from being the first Torah instruction to becoming a running theme throughout the history of our people.

## THE MATRIARCHS

The Torah tells many stories. These stories and the way in which they are recounted also serve the purpose of Torah itself: *hora'ah*, teaching. As the Torah recounts the beginnings of the Jewish people, the theme of childbirth is once again central.

The Torah describes with great pathos the longing to bear children that each of the Matriarchs felt. Sarah, Rivkah, and Rachel were childless for many years. They prayed, yearned, demanded, and did everything in their power to merit the blessing of children. As described in the Torah, the terminology they used left no room for doubt that childbearing touched the very core of their being. Doubting Avraham's devotion to this cause, Sarah exclaimed, "May the L-rd judge between me and you!"[9] Rachel, in her anguish, said to Yaakov, "Give me children, and if not, I am dead!"[10]

The story of the birth of Yitzchak is the Torah reading for Rosh Hashanah. Following this, we read the poignant story of Chanah. Chanah had no children, and the story tells of her longing and intense prayer to be granted a child. After conceiving and giving birth to Shmuel, her tremendous elation found expression in her prophetic song of praise to G-d. The fact that these readings are chosen to be read on the first day, or "head," of the year, demonstrates the centrality of these narratives to Jewish life. It is with these stories that the Torah seeks to shape our own approach to the birth of all Jewish children—firstborn and additional children alike.

As far as our subject is concerned, what turns out to be most fascinating is the story of Leah. Leah was the only one of the four Matriarchs who had no trouble conceiving initially. On the contrary, G-d "opened her womb," and she ended up having more children than all the other Matriarchs combined.[11]

---

9    Ibid., 16:5.
10   Ibid., 30:1.
11   Ibid., 29:31.

As the Torah recounts the birth of Leah's children, it describes her ever-growing exuberance and joy with every additional child she birthed. Moreover, after her fourth child, Yehudah, was born, she stopped giving birth. Knowing that more children were destined to be born to Yaakov,[12] she gave her maidservant, Zilpah, to her husband for marriage, so that she might merit bearing more of Yaakov's sons. Leah's desire was fulfilled with the birth of her two additional sons, Yissachar and Zevulun.

Much of Leah's elation found expression in the fact that, because of their many joint children, her husband, Yaakov, would now have a special bond with her. Leah felt inferior in the marriage to her sister Rachel, who was Yaakov's initial choice. The verse tells us that this was indeed the reason why G-d gave her many children.[13] In Leah's words, her many children would cause Yaakov to be "attached" to her (the meaning behind the name of her third son, Levi),[14] or even more so, that Yaakov would make his principal dwelling with her (the meaning in the name of her sixth son, Zevulun).[15]

In summary, the Torah's account of Leah is the greatest counter-narrative to the notion that numerous children are "extra" or "burdensome." To Leah, the very opposite was true: each additional child increased her joy and gratitude even further. This joy was indeed shared with her husband Yaakov, whose bond with his wife Leah deepened with each additional child she had.

## TOTAL DEVOTION

As the Torah continues to chronicle the story of the Jewish people, the stories of devotion to having children climb to the most intense of proportions.

This begins with the description of the Jewish sojourn in Egypt: "The Israelites were fertile and prolific; they multiplied and increased

---

12    See ibid., 30:21; *Rashi* ad loc.
13    Ibid., 29:31.
14    Ibid., 29:34.
15    Ibid., 30:20.

very greatly, so that the land was filled with them."[16] Even prior to their enslavement, being in Egypt—a foreign and debased land—would have seemed very far from the ideal place to have and raise children. This was, as the Torah describes, after Yosef and his entire generation already passed, leaving the Israelites vulnerable to what later became a bitter exile. But G-d's blessing, and the commitment of Jewish parents to receive it, took on its fullest dimension specifically in Egypt. Notwithstanding all the obvious difficulties, the Jewish family flourished.

The climax, however, was yet to come. The commitment to having children would soon take on the form of complete self-sacrifice.

Fearing the bold increase of the Jewish population, Pharaoh and his advisers sought ways to curtail it. After failing to enlist the Jewish midwives in murdering the newborn boys, Pharaoh decreed, "Every boy that is born you shall throw into the Nile, but let every girl live."[17] (*Rashi*, quoting the midrash, explains that Pharaoh "was particular only about the male children because his astrologers told him that there was to be born to a Hebrew woman a son who would become their deliverer.")[18]

Immediately afterwards, the Torah begins recounting the story of the birth of Moshe. The Talmud, however, fills us in on the dramatic events that took place in the interim:

> *Amram, the father of Moshe, was the great man of his generation. Once he saw that the wicked Pharaoh said, "Every boy that is born you shall throw into the Nile, but let every girl live," he said, "We are laboring for nothing (by bringing children into the world to be killed)." He therefore arose and divorced his wife. All others who saw this followed his example: they arose and divorced their wives.*
>
> *His daughter, Miriam, said to him: "Father, your decree is harsher than that of Pharaoh! Pharaoh decreed only regarding*

---

16    *Shemos* 1:7.

17    Ibid., 1:16.

18    Ibid.

*the males, but you decreed both on the males and on the females (for now no children will be born at all)! Additionally, Pharaoh decreed to kill them only in this world, but you decreed in this world and in the World to Come (as those not born will not enter the World to Come). Additionally, concerning the wicked Pharaoh, it is uncertain whether his decree will be fulfilled. You are a righteous person, and as such, your decrees will certainly be fulfilled." Amram accepted his daughter's words. He arose and remarried his wife. All the others who saw this followed his example: they arose and remarried their wives.*[19]

The pure and uncompromising faith of a small child, and the deep commitment of her parents and adult peers to follow her, paid off. While Miriam did have a point, there was also no small case to be made for her father's original position. Still, Miriam would not succumb to what seemed like a rational argument. All she knew was that the Jewish people had to continue despite all odds. It was this display of unwavering *emunah*, faith and trust in G-d, that brought about the first stage of the ultimate redemption: the birth of Moshe.

The Talmud tells us that Amram and Yocheved did not remarry in a halfhearted or begrudging manner. The Talmud observes the wording of the verse: "And a man of the house of Levi went, and took as a wife a daughter of Levi."[20] The Talmud asks:

*Since Yocheved had already been married to Amram for some years (Miriam and Aharon were already born), the verse should have stated: "And he took her back as a wife." Rav Yehudah bar Zevida says: The wording of the verse teaches that Amram performed for her a formal act of marriage, as though he were marrying her for the first time. He seated her in a bridal palanquin (appiryon), Aharon and Miriam sang before her, and the ministering angels said, "A joyful mother of children."*[21]

---

19   *Sotah* 12a.
20   *Shemos* 2:1.
21   *Sotah* 12a.

This initial act of faith was eventually put to the test. After giving birth to Moshe, Yocheved was compelled to place him in a basket afloat the Nile river. The Talmud records the riveting story of that fateful day.[22] Miriam, as a child, had prophesied that her mother would beget a son that would be the Jewish savior. When Moshe was put into the Nile, her father, Amram, stood up and tapped her on the head. "Where is your prophecy?" he demanded. As the Torah recounts, Moshe was miraculously saved by none other than the daughter of Pharaoh himself.

This was the story around the birth of Moshe. The Talmud tells us that similar miracles were experienced by the rest of the people. This, again, was in response to the steadfast faith displayed in particular by the Jewish women:

> *Rav Avira taught: In the merit of the righteous women that were in that generation, the Jewish people were redeemed from Egypt. At the time when these women would go to the river to draw water, the Holy One Blessed Be He would send them small fish that would enter into their pitchers, and they would draw pitchers that were half filled with water and half filled with fish.*
>
> *They would then come [home] and place two pots on the fire; one pot of hot water for washing their husbands, and one pot of fish with which to feed them. They would then take what they prepared to the field. They would bathe their husbands, anoint them with oil, feed them the fish, give them to drink, and bond with them in marital relations between the borders and fences of the fields.*
>
> *When these women would become pregnant, they would come back to their homes. When the time came, they would go and give birth in the field under the apple tree, as it is stated: "Under the apple tree I awakened you. There your mother was in travail with you; there was she in travail and brought you forth" (Shir Hashirim 8:5).*

---

22   Ibid., 13a.

*The Holy One Blessed Be He would send from the Heavens above an angel who would clean and prepare the newborns, just as a midwife prepares the newborn, as it is stated: "And as for your birth, on the day you were born, your navel was not cut nor were you washed with water for cleansing; you were not salted at all, nor swaddled at all" (Yechezkel 16:4).*

*The angel would gather for them two round stones from the field and the babies would nurse from that which would flow out of them. One of the stones flowed with oil and one of the stones flowed with honey, as it is stated: "And He would suckle them with honey from a crag and oil from a flinty rock" (Devarim 32:13).*

*When the Egyptians would notice the Jewish babies, they would come to kill them. But a miracle would occur and the babies would be absorbed by the earth. The Egyptians would bring oxen and plow upon them, as it is stated: "The plowers plowed upon my back; they made long their furrows" (Tehillim 129:3). After the Egyptians would leave, the babies would emerge and exit the ground like grass of the field, as it is stated: "I caused you to increase even as the growth of the field" (Yechezkel 16:7).*

*Once the babies would grow, they would come like many flocks of sheep to their homes, as it is stated in the continuation of the verse: "And you did increase and grow up and you came with excellent beauty (ba'adi adayim)" (Yechezkel 16:7). Do not read the verse as "ba'adi adayim—with excellent beauty," rather, read it as "be'edrei adarim—as many flocks."*

*When the Holy One Blessed Be He revealed Himself at the Red Sea, these children recognized Him first, as it is stated: "This is my G-d, and I will glorify Him" (Shemos 15:2).*[23]

As quoted above, the Jews multiplied intensely even before the time of slavery. The midrash (quoted by *Rashi*) tells us that Jewish women

---

23    Ibid., 11b.

would give birth to six babies at a time![24] Then, at the time of the slavery itself, not only did the childbirth not diminish, it intensified: "As much as they would afflict them, so did they multiply, and so did they gain strength."[25]

It is worthy of noting that Moshe was born to his parents after they had already fulfilled what is characterized in many places as the minimum number of children to fulfill the mitzvah of childbearing. The birth of Moshe was preceded by Miriam and Aharon, namely, a girl and a boy.[26] Coupled with the terrible situation created by Pharaoh's decree, Moshe's parents—as well as the entire people who followed them—could have cited some strong basis for at least curtailing their family to a minimum number of children.

But, evidently, this option was not on the table. In the case of Moshe's parents, such a consideration would have meant that the redeemer of the Jewish people, the greatest prophet ever to live, would never have been born.

## A REWARD FOR A TROUBLED MARRIAGE

The Torah's approach to childbirth as a blessing also comes across in the Torah's matter-of-fact narration. One such occasion appears in the portion dedicated to the laws of *sotah*—the woman suspected of adultery. In Biblical times, a woman who was suspected of adultery would go through a prescribed test of drinking the waters of *sotah*, which would miraculously determine if she was guilty or not. If she was in fact guilty, the water would act like a poison to her and she (together with her fellow sinner) would die. If, however, she was innocent, the water would bring her great blessing: "She shall be exempted and bear seed."[27]

*Rashi*, quoting the Talmud, explains that this blessing of "seed" applied to many aspects of childbearing: "If she used to have painful

---

24    *Shemos Rabbah* 1:8. See also *Ibn Ezra, Shemos* ibid., 7.
25    *Shemos* 1:12.
26    See footnotes in introduction above.
27    *Bamidbar* 5:28.

births, she would now have easy births; if she used to give birth to ugly children, she would now bear beautiful ones."[28]

This is an incredibly powerful statement. Consider that, the case of a *sotah* is not that of a very blissful, harmonious marriage. For whatever reason, the husband suspects his wife of having an affair with another man and warns her against being alone with him. This is something that would hardly happen had their marriage been healthy in the first place. After the woman continues to meet the other man but denies any misconduct, the test of the *sotah* is administered to determine if she is in fact innocent or not.

The Torah states that the reward for the degradation of the innocent *sotah* concerns the bearing of children. In other words, additional children are a blessing. They are in fact the very blessing that could *heal* a marriage, even one as troubled as that of a *sotah*.

Here again, the verse which speaks of the blessing to the innocent *sotah* does not concern itself with whether she had any children until then, or how many she had. As the Talmud explains it, it is talking primarily of a woman who had children already, and the blessing was that she would consequently have more children—only now with more ease and more beauty than before.

## A BLESSING

Throughout the Torah, having many children is described as being a blessing and a cause for happiness: "And G-d *blessed* them, and G-d said to them, 'Be fruitful and multiply.'"[29] Yaakov, when presenting his large family to his brother Eisav, said: "The children with whom G-d has favored your servant."[30]

The Torah always describes the increase of children as an increase in blessing. In His words to both Avraham and Yaakov, G-d promises them that their "seed" shall be "as the stars of the heaven" or "as the dust of

---

28    See ibid., 26a.
29    *Bereishis* 1:28.
30    Ibid., 33:5.

the earth."[31] In their parting words to their daughter and sister, Rivkah, her mother and brother bless her, saying: "May you become thousands of myriads."[32] Yaakov finishes his blessing to his grandchildren, Menasheh and Ephraim, with: "May they multiply abundantly like fish, in the midst of the land."[33] Moshe, in his final words to the Israelites, blesses them, saying: "May Hashem, the G-d of your fathers, increase your numbers a thousandfold, and bless you as He promised you."[34]

This same approach is followed with many examples in the Tanach, Talmud, midrash, and the long history of Rabbinic literature.[35]

> *Behold! The heritage of G-d is children; a reward—is the fruit of the womb. Like arrows in the hand of a warrior, so are children of youth. Praiseworthy is the man who fills his quiver with them..."*[36]

The Torah sees the joy in having children as so basic and fundamental that it speaks of it as a self-understood fact. To be sure, such matter-of-fact narration is yet another one of the ways which the Torah chooses to convey its messages. The lack of spelled-out instruction does not diminish the importance of a matter. On the contrary, where applicable, it only emphasizes how basic and necessary it is.[37]

---

31    Ibid., 22:17; 28:14.

32    Ibid., 24:60.

33    Ibid., 48:16.

34    *Devarim* 1:11.

35    See for example: *Tehillim* 128:3-4; *Iyov* 42:12-13; *Berachos* 63b; *Shabbos* 30b; *Temurah* 16a.

36    *Tehillim*, 127:3-5. See *Radak*, *Sforno*, and commentary by Rabbi S.R. Hirsch ad loc.

37    One other example of this is marriage. The Torah tells the story of how Chavah was "separated" from Adam while he was sleeping, and that after this, Adam recognized that she was "bone of my bones and flesh of my flesh." The Torah then comments in conclusion: "Therefore, a man shall leave his father and his mother and cleave to his wife, and they shall become one flesh" (*Bereishis* 2:24). It is quite clear from this matter-of-fact narrative that the Torah sees marriage as the natural and imperative status for the human being. In fact, when it comes to the various commandments associated with marriage, the Torah does not actually contain a command to get married! The legal obligation to marry emerges only by virtue of the fact that the Torah obligates a man to have children but also prohibits intimacy out of wedlock.

# CHAPTER 3

# Ultimate Issues

## THE BIG QUESTION

Thus far we have demonstrated how, throughout the Torah, the continuity of having children is viewed as highly important and a colossal blessing. To the modern mind, however, this is something increasingly difficult to identify with.

What is so important about having another child? Can we articulate this great blessing the Torah speaks of? Does it apply in our day and age?

To begin this discussion, we must take a step back.

The question of having *additional* children assumes that there is a satisfactory answer to the more fundamental question, namely, "Why have children at all?" After all, a reason that is compelling enough for having the first child should likely have some bearing on whether to have an additional one, and another after that.

Admittedly, from a subjective parental perspective, this is not really the case. Without entering the discussion of whether we are biologically conditioned to desire progeny, we can still assert with confidence that this need, if it exists, is satisfied by either one or few children. This is surely true if we visit the various physiological, emotional, and sociological explanations given by the average person to explain the need they feel to have children. The statistics, in this sense, speak for themselves: today, people of every background, culture, and race are opting for fewer children. If the approach to having children is subjective, namely, that the discussion is centered merely around the need of parents to have children, an indefinite increase in family size is indeed hard to justify.

Now, this is not to say that there are no benefits to having many children. On the contrary, as will be elaborated upon in the Part 2 of this book, the benefits of a large family are strong and many. This discussion, however, is at the fundamental level. What if we were to ask the question from an *objective* perspective? Is there a case to be made for this potential child to be born? And if so, what is it?

A closer analysis of this question brings us to the biggest question of all. Justifying *re*production can only come about once we can justify the product itself. If the creation of the human being himself can be justified and explained, chances are we may be able to carry it over into the creation of additional people.

Arriving at such an explanation from a secular viewpoint will be quite difficult, if not impossible. Secular disciplines, by definition, deal with the examination and analysis of nature. They cannot, however, be an authority as to the meaning of it. Physicality does not disclose anything about its meaning; all it "says" is, "I am here." The study of the universe reveals much about *how* it operates but does not address the question of *why* we are here. Insofar as man is concerned, science and philosophy can describe the benefits of man to the world, but it will be overreaching itself in the attempt to explain why these benefits to the world, or the world altogether, are necessary. For the meaning of Creation to be known, we must have access to the Creator.

## THE PLAN FOR MAN

Before the Torah lays out the injunction to create *additional* human beings ("be fruitful and multiply"), the Torah recounts in great detail the story of how G-d created the prototypes—Adam and Chavah. An examination of the sources around this text reveal that it is precisely here that an immense drama unfolds: *Why did G-d create man?*

In the first week of Creation, all seems to be going exceptionally well. G-d created light and darkness, the sky and the sea, vegetation and animal life; a magnificent universe all found to be "good."[1] Finally, G-d said, "Let us make man in our image, after our likeness...And G-d created man in His image, in the image of G-d He created him, male and female He created them."[2]

The Talmud explains that the statement "Let *us* make man" was directed toward the Heavenly angels. The angels, however, were actually completely opposed to the entire idea:

> When the Holy One Blessed Be He came to create man, He created a group of ministering angels and asked them, "Do you agree that we should make man in our image?"
>
> They replied, "Sovereign of the Universe, what will be his deeds?"
>
> G-d showed them the history of mankind.
>
> The angels replied, "What is man that You are mindful of him?" [In other words, let man not be created.] G-d destroyed the angels.
>
> He created a second group and asked them the same question, and they gave the same answer. G-d destroyed them.
>
> He created a third group of angels, and they replied, "Sovereign of the Universe, the first and second group of angels told You not to create man, and it did not avail them. You did not listen. What then can we say but this: The universe is Yours. Do with it as You wish."
>
> And G-d created man.
>
> When it came to the generation of the Flood, and then to the generation of those who built the Tower of Babel, the angels

---

1   The description of creation being "good" is repeated six times throughout the Creation narrative in the first chapter of *Bereishis*.

2   *Bereishis* 1:26–27.

> *said to G-d, "Were not the first angels right? See how great*
> *is the corruption of mankind." G-d replied, "Even to old age,*
> *I will not change, and even to grey hair, I will sustain you"*
> *(Yeshayahu 46:4).³*

What emerges from this puzzling yet telling narrative is that the creation of man defied even the logic of Heavenly beings. This creation that G-d intended—man—could make use of his free will to wreak havoc in the beautiful world G-d created. To the angels, the creation of man was not a risk worth taking. To G-d, however, it was.

In Jewish tradition, our Sages actually spent much time agonizing over this very question. Fascinatingly, they too came to a similar conclusion, not much different than their angelic counterparts:

> *For two and a half years the house of Shammai and the house*
> *of Hillel argued.*
>
> *These said: Better for man never to have been created than to*
> *have been created. And these said: Better for man to have been*
> *created than not to have been created.*
>
> *They counted and decided: Better for man never to have been*
> *created than to have been created.*
>
> *Now that he has been created, he should examine his actions.⁴*

Although their reasons were quite different from modern perspectives, the Talmudic Sages, too, found it difficult to justify the existence of man. It seems that things would just have been a lot better if man had not been necessary in the first place. From the Talmudic point of view, since man was likely to do more harm than good, better not to take the risk! Of course, now that we are here, they said, we should make the best of it.

The question begs for an explanation: Why indeed? If it is "better for man never to have been created," why did G-d insist on this idea?

---

3    *Sanhedrin* 38b.
4    *Eruvin* 13b.

What kind of plan was this if time and again the actions of man, or the lack thereof, would justify his discontinuation or destruction? It seems that no one, neither angel nor man himself, is able to wrap their mind around this. Why did G-d do this?

Arguably, it is the world that would have been missing its key component were it not to include the creation of mankind. But this only shifts the question as to the purpose of the world itself—with or without man. Moreover, it does not answer the question as to why G-d created man in the way He did, with all his shortcomings and fallacies.

Kabbalistic and Chassidic teachings choose to address the question from the perspective of the soul of man. The soul is described as something G-dly, a part of G-d. Before its descent, the soul "stands in the presence of G-d."[5] It experiences and comprehends G-dliness. G-dliness is real to it. The sojourn of the soul in the physical world is for a temporary time, after which the "spirit returns to G-d Who gave it."[6] As a G-dly being, it is an incredible descent and a painful experience for the soul to live in a physical and material world so devoid of G-dliness.

Anyone who has experienced spiritual elevation, even for a short amount of time, can attest to the acute feeling of bleakness accompanying the return into the material, mundane world. Such feeling is just a taste of what the soul goes through. Physical reality is completely alien to this G-dly being. It can be compared, at least somewhat, to a wise and refined person having to live among backwards and coarse peasants.

The tragedy is even greater when a person chooses to spend their entire life submerged in the physical. As they plod through the various stages of the few short years we call a lifetime, they may never be aware that their soul—their very self—belongs to a reality so very different and higher than the one in which they are living.

Moreover, living in this world means not only feeling more at home with the G-dless, it means experiencing never-ending temptations and challenges to keep morally and spiritually afloat. The soul, prior to its descent, lives in an entirely G-dly existence without the experience of

---

5    See *Zohar* 3:104b; ibid., 1:190b.

6    *Koheles* 12:7.

anything contrary to this. The question, in this sense, is not so much philosophical as it is emotional: Why must the soul descend to earth?

Understanding this underlying issue is crucial to our discussion, as the Talmud states: "There are three partners in the creation of man: the father, the mother, and G-d."[7] G-d decided that the reproduction of man would necessitate two other parties without whom it would not come to be. Indeed, not only was man given the ability to manipulate the rest of creation, he was even given the choice of whether or not to continue his own existence!

In this vein, the very same question that is asked with regard to G-d creating the first man could be, and should be, asked by man himself with regard to his own reproduction: Why? Why begin with all of this? Why should *I* bring a soul down to this world?

---

7   *Kiddushin* 30b.

# CHAPTER 4

# *Destiny*

## GAN EDEN

The conventional rationalization for the creation of man—or the descent of the soul to this earth—is that it is a descent for the purpose of an ascent. It is an investment of an initial loss for the purpose of a greater gain. Man labors here on earth for a certain period of time, and upon returning to his Maker, he is rewarded for the good deeds he performed. The reward in Gan Eden, the world of the souls, is in the form of revelation of G-dliness—a goodness and pleasure in relation to which all earthly pleasures and rewards pale in significance.[1]

Taken at its surface, there is an inherent problem with this understanding. The existence described above is exactly the kind of situation in which the soul finds itself prior to its descent! Before the soul comes to this world, it exists in its natural state of being—a G-dly state. To use a phrase from the Talmud, "One who buys and sells at the same price—is he called a merchant?"[2]

---

1 See *Rambam Hilchos Teshuvah*, chap. 8.
2 See *Bava Metzia* 40b.

35

What justifies the creation of man simply for him to return to the same state in which he was before?

The crucial answer is that the level of G-dly connection and experience enabled by the descent to this world is completely unparalleled to that which the soul can experience prior to its descent. What we can reach afterwards far surpasses anything we could have experienced before.

## TESHUVAH

When it comes to the concept of repentance, or *teshuvah*, a simple question may be asked: What brings a person to do *teshuvah*? If sin is something he does not want to do, he would never have done it in the first place. Evidently, he decided that going against G-d does not bother him. That is why he sinned. So why is he now doing *teshuvah*?

The obvious answer is that, in truth, a Jew never actually wants to sin. Sin is something that runs contrary to the truth and essence of the Jew. Our essence, our true selves, is one with G-d. This can never and will never change. This is who we are. It is merely that a "spirit of foolishness"[3] sometimes overcomes us and we succumb to temptation. *Teshuvah* is the revelation and return to our inner selves. *Teshuvah* is when our inner self comes to the fore.

Now, this revelation of our true selves does not depend on sinning. Every time a Jew overcomes a spiritual challenge in this world, large or small, what is ultimately operative is the fact that the soul cannot allow for sin to occur to it. G-dliness is its very life, and anything contrary to G-dliness is, to the soul, death. Being righteous is basically a question of how much a person allows his inner G-dly self to shine.

What is true, however, is that it takes an encounter with the *opposite* of G-dliness to bring out how our true essence is inseverable from G-d. Had we never encountered evil, there would be nothing to bring out our inner core. This rule is applicable in every facet of life: leave a person unchallenged and you will never see or feel what they are really all about.

---

3    See *Sotah* 3b.

This is the explanation behind the Talmudic statement, "In the place that a *baal teshuvah* [one who has done *teshuvah*] stands, even the perfectly righteous do not stand."[4] Without challenge, even the loftiest level of righteous character is ultimately limited. The *baal teshuvah*, however, does not serve G-d on the terms of his own character; on the contrary, this character of his has failed. The *baal teshuvah* brings out his soul. The soul is infinite. The soul is G-dly. In other words, *teshuvah* is the move from the limitation of our own character to the experience of our unlimited soul.

On a broader scale, this is exactly what transpires with the soul itself through its descent to this world. While it is on High, the soul is never confronted with anything unG-dly. That the soul is a G-dly being with an infinite and unbreakable connection to G-d—this lies dormant.

The challenges and difficulties of this world take the soul out of its comfort zone. Once it finds itself in an unholy and unG-dly world, the soul must change gear. Were it to remain in the relatively passive state it was in before its descent, the soul would drown in the tidal wave of physicality and materialism. What emerges here in this world is that the soul, when tested, is infinitely strong. No force whatsoever can overpower this G-dly soul.

The ultimate example of this is how Jews throughout the ages gave up their lives "*al kiddush Hashem*, for the sanctity of G-d's name." Very often, these were simple and unlearned Jews. But their soul was alive. There was nothing and no one that could possibly move them from their Jewishness.

It is only in this world that the soul can realize its own infinite potential. As a result of its life in this world, the soul is a changed being. Life in this world allows the soul to experience its truly unlimited G-dly self.

## A DWELLING FOR G-D

The explanation above is often offered as the ultimate purpose for the creation of man. Other sources, however, take it a step further.

---

4    *Berachos* 34b.

The primary objective in creating the world is characterized in the words of the midrash: "G-d desired to dwell in the lowest of realms."[5] G-d wants this physical world, not as a means to an end, but as His primary objective. The world is to become His "dwelling," the place of His ultimate belonging.

To achieve this, the soul is sent down to this world. By virtue of being a G-dly being, the soul is capable of being a conductor for G-dliness, bringing G-dliness into its own human self and into the world around it. This is done through the study of Torah and fulfillment of mitzvos. Studying Torah or fulfilling a mitzvah imbues and permeates the world with G-dliness, thus transforming it into a place for G-d.

The complete fulfillment of this objective will be the coming of Mashiach. In the days of Mashiach, the cumulative effort of making this world a place for G-d will be realized and revealed. At this time, not only will the physical world bring out and exude G-dliness, but it will become the place where G-d Himself is revealed and evident.

Now, this is extraordinary. The natural fabric of the physical world is such that it obstructs G-dly revelation. This is the entire difference between the physical and the spiritual. The spiritual is the consciousness of something higher. The physical is the obstruction of anything beyond itself. Although G-d is everywhere, it is nevertheless possible to live in this world and not feel or sense G-d at all. By its obstruction of G-dliness, the physical world facilitates much of that which is antithetical to G-dliness.

For G-dliness to be expressed by the physical, or moreover, for it to be the place for G-d Himself to dwell, should be impossible. Logically, there is no potential for this. Physicality is supposed to block spirituality. Even if some goodness or holiness is introduced to the physical, the physical must remain an obstruction to G-dliness if it is to remain physical. If the physical begins to reveal something higher than itself, then it becomes some kind of a spiritual world. It cannot be both.

How is such a total transformation even possible?

---

5   See *Midrash Tanchuma Naso* 16 and *Bechukosai* 3; *Bereishis Rabbah* 3; *Bamidbar Rabbah* 13:6.

The truth is that the ability to transform the unG-dly into a G-d-worthy place lies only within the Creator Himself. Only He Who has no limitation or boundary can achieve this. The fact that a Jew can influence such change is only because the Jew connects with G-d Who has no limitations.

Even the unlimited connection of the soul to its Creator brought to the fore with the experience of *teshuvah* is still a revelation of the potential strength that lies within the soul itself. It is a revelation of the unlimited energy contained *within* its own potential, but not anything that *defies* potential. Put a little differently, it is a revelation that answers to the rules of convention—in this case, the convention of the soul's infinite essence. Infinity, however, also has a convention—it is infinite. Infinity dictates that it, and the finite, are incurably separate. The finite will never be able to be a place for the infinite. Even with all its unlimited G-dly connection, the soul will never have the ability to make the physical world the place for G-d.

Imbuing the physical with G-dliness necessitates elevation and access to a connection with G-d that goes beyond all convention and rules. By descending to earth, the soul enters the kind of unlimited connection with G-d which defies all convention and rules.

## THE REWARD

The World to Come is the world of truth where G-dliness is revealed and apparent. It is here that the soul experiences that which it achieved on earth.

Upon concluding its time on earth, the soul is a transformed being. As we have described, the soul is extracted from its limited self and elevated to a limitless and boundless bond with G-d. One element of this transformation is that the soul is capable of continually rising to levels completely beyond its previous spiritual capacity.

Before its descent to this world, the soul is described as "standing before G-d."[6] The term "standing" is used intentionally. It describes the

---

6    See *Zohar*, vol. 1, 233b and vol. 3, 104b.

fact that the soul, like all other creations, has its own specific spiritual nature before its descent. In this sense, it is similar to the angels on High, each of whom has their own G-dly function. After its time in this world, the soul is given "strides among these [angels] who stand here."[7] The soul now ascends to completely new levels of comprehension and experience of the Divine. This expresses the fact that the soul has now broken out of its defined status and entered the world of the infinite. There are now no limits to the spiritual heights and levels it can attain.

## THE BIG PICTURE

The reward for the soul after its descent to this world is indeed a great one. But then again, G-d, in His essence, is incomprehensible and impossible to experience. Any comprehension or experience takes in a concept, an idea, or a feeling—and that is exactly what G-d Himself is not. Even the previously described achievement of a connection to G-d that defies rules and convention still does not mean that the soul has now touched the essence of G-d Himself. G-d is untouchable.

The creation of man, however, achieves the greatest thing of all. The ultimate purpose in the creation of man is described in the words of the Mishnah: "I have been created to serve my Maker."[8] The creation of man is something for G-d. As we have explained, G-d—in His essence and totality—desires this physical world as His place. We have the privilege of making it happen.

The greatness in being a part of this surpasses any other of the achievements described above.

Nothing that the soul can ever do will allow it to reach G-d Himself. G-d Himself, however, desires this world to be His place. By becoming a part of this endeavor, the soul, or man, becomes included and attached with G-d Himself.

The belonging and revelation of G-d in this world will be fully realized in the time of Mashiach—especially in the time of the resurrection

---

7   *Zechariah* 3:7.

8   *Kiddushin* 82b.

of the dead, when the soul will be reunited with the body. G-d Himself will then be evident and in this physical world, and the physical person will become united and one with G-d Himself.

Moreover, this union with G-d Himself will take place with the soul being clothed once again in the physical body. The body—the partner of the soul on this earth—cannot join the soul in the G-dly experience of Gan Eden. In the words of G-d to Moshe, "Man shall not see Me and live."[9] The experience of G-dliness is completely beyond the world of the physical, which is why the soul must leave the body in order to enter any level of G-dly consciousness.

G-d Himself, however, is the truth and essence of everything. He is not limited in any setting, physical nor spiritual. G-d Himself chooses the physical to be His ultimate place of belonging. It will be the Jew, in his or her return to the physical body, that will realize this final intention.

## THE MEANING OF ANOTHER CHILD

In summary, in light of the above, we can state that there is nothing that can remotely parallel the greatness that lies in the creation of man on earth. It constitutes the arrival at the be-all and end-all of everything—absolutely everything:

- For the soul of man, it is the entry into an infinite and boundless connection with G-dliness.
- Chiefly however, the creation of man enables him to fulfill G-d's purpose in creation—that G-d Himself dwell and "belong" in the physical world. By being included in this, the Jew enters a connection with G-d Himself, and, with the coming of Mashiach, the physical Jew—body and soul together—will be the place of G-d's final and complete dwelling.

Our Sages tell us that, indeed, although it is a tremendous descent and involves great difficulty, the soul on High deeply anticipates the time when it will be given the chance to descend to this world.

---

9    *Shemos* 33:20.

Somehow, the soul knows and feels the significance of the journey it must take.

Having said all this, there is still an additional element that is crucial to this conversation. True, one may say, there may be incredible *significance* in the birth of another child. But, after all, there is a difference between significance and *necessity*.

Our next chapter will examine the sources which establish the idea that the birth of an additional child is not just a nicety (to the degree we can call it that). The truth is that the entire plan of creation hinges on bringing another Jewish child into the world.

CHAPTER 5

# One Child—Every Child

## AN ENTIRE WORLD

As explained earlier, the Jewish people were given the Torah and, with this, charged with carrying out the Divine purpose of creation. The Jewish people are subdivided into many individual souls. Each individual Jew has a part in fulfilling the function of the Jewish people at large. The purpose of creation is fulfilled with a collaborative effort of all Jews of all time. In other words, the descent of every individual soul to this world and the fulfillment of its specific mission in this world is *indispensable.*

The midrash tells us that had one Jew been missing at the time the Torah was given, the entire event would have been impossible. G-d would have not come down at Sinai or given the Torah at all.[1] Indeed, the midrash also tells us that not only was every living Jew present at Sinai, but each and every Jewish soul of all future generations was present as well.[2]

---

1    *Mechilta Yisro* 19:11; *Devarim Rabbah* 7:8.
2    *Pirkei D'Rabbi Eliezer*, 41; *Shemos Rabbah* 28:6.

The opening words of G-d at this event were, "I am the L-rd *thy* G-d." Modern English translates the Hebrew as "your G-d," but this, in effect, is misleading, as the word "you" can indicate either singular or plural. G-d actually uttered the Ten Commandments in the singular, as He spoke to every Jew individually: "When the Holy One Blessed Be He spoke, each Jew said 'It is with me that the speech is being spoken.'"[3]

This is not just a quaint idea. The entire purpose of creation, set in motion with the giving of the Torah, rests entirely on each individual Jew doing their part.

The Torah was given with the most immense drama. Moshe, Aharon, the seventy elders, and the entire people who had just witnessed the Exodus all stood in total awe. The entire cosmos stood still watching as G-d spoke privately to each individual Jewish child—*including the one who, after thousands of years, is now ready to be conceived.*

The essential contribution of each individual to the fulfillment of the Divine purpose is expressed in several areas. One of the most major ones appears in the laws of *teshuvah* by Maimonides who says something incredible:

> *A person should always look at himself as equally balanced between merit and sin, and the world as equally balanced between merit and sin. If he performs one sin, he tips his balance and that of the entire world to the side of guilt and brings destruction upon himself.*
>
> *[On the other hand,] if he performs one mitzvah, he tips his balance and that of the entire world to the side of merit and brings deliverance and salvation to himself and others. This is implied by [Mishlei 10:25] "A righteous man is the foundation of the world," i.e., he who acted righteously tipped the balance of the entire world to merit and saved it."[4]*

---

3   *Yalkut Shimoni Yisro* 20:2.

4   *Rambam, Hilchos Teshuvah* 3:4.

On the face of it, this would seem perplexing: Why would the deeds of one individual have a bearing on the destiny of the entire world?

The rationale behind this idea rests on the principle above—each individual and the good deeds they perform constitute an integral part in the Divine project. No one and nothing is redundant. Each movement carries ultimate significance.

If this applies to the *actions* of the individual, it is obviously amplified when speaking about the *existence* of each person.

In conclusion, the Torah's position can be summarized using the emphatic words of our Sages:

> *It was for this reason that man was first created as one person: to teach that anyone who causes one Jewish life to be lost, is accounted for in Scripture as if he caused a whole world to be lost; and anyone who sustains one Jewish life, Scripture accounts to him as if he sustained an entire world…A man strikes many coins from the same die, and all the coins are alike. But the King, the King of Kings, the Holy One Blessed Be He strikes every man from the die of the first man, and yet no man is quite like his fellow. Therefore, every person must say, "For my sake the world was created.*[5]

This concept is what lies beneath the passage in the Talmud that states: "The Son of David will not come before all the souls in *Guf* will have been disposed of."[6] The "Son of David" is the Talmudic way of referring to Mashiach. The term *Guf* (literally, "body") is a reference to the spiritual realm inhabited by the souls of the yet unborn.

As explained, the coming of Mashiach is the result and sum total of the accumulative effort in making this world a dwelling place for G-d. At that time, the desire of G-d to belong and be revealed in the physical world will be realized. Any individual soul that is prevented from coming down to this earth prevents part of G-d's grand plan for Creation from being realized.

---

5    *Mishnah Sanhedrin* 4:5.
6    *Niddah* 13b.

The birth of every additional Jew is a joy, not only for the family—or even for the generation—into which they are born. The joy is for all generations and every being brought into existence by G-d, as the fulfillment of G-d's plan in creation depends on each individual soul doing its part. Far from being a private matter, the decision of bringing another Jewish life into this world has a bearing on the entire past, present, and future of both the Jewish people and of the world at large: "Just as the children of Israel were redeemed from Egypt in the merit that they were fruitful and multiplied, so too will they be redeemed in time to come in the merit that they will be fruitful and multiply."[7]

What we have learned so far leads to the conclusive Jewish approach to the question of having additional children:

> *Although a man has fulfilled the mitzvah of being fruitful and multiplying, he is bound by a Rabbinic commandment not to refrain from being fruitful and multiplying as long as he is physically potent. For anyone who adds a soul to the Jewish people is considered as if he built an entire world.*[8]

The Divine intention in creation depends on every single Jew taking his or her part in fulfilling it. Tampering with a single life is tampering with the destiny of the entire creation. Sustaining—let alone facilitating—just a single life in this world is an act upon which the entire purpose of creation rests.

All the above is endlessly magnified by the fact that this one child contains the potential of bringing about an *infinite* number of descendants—literally "an entire world."[9]

Aside from the indispensable value of each individual, there is also an element of quality at play. When speaking of the obligation to continue having children, the Talmud[10] quotes the words of King Solomon: "Sow

---

7    *Tanna D'bei Eliyahu Zuta*, chap. 14.

8    *Rambam Hilchos Ishut* 15:16.

9    In some sources, this idea is used to explain the Mishnaic statement, "Anyone who sustains one Jewish life, Scripture accounts to him as if he sustained an entire world." See *Hayom Yom*, Elul 16.

10    *Yevamos* 62b.

your seed in the morning, and don't hold back your hand in the evening, since you don't know which is going to succeed, the one or the other, or if both are equally good."[11]

One can never know what this yet unborn child may achieve in his or her lifetime. What cosmic, spiritual changes certain individuals achieve is obviously beyond our scope as mortals. But even from our simple point of view, some of history's greatest achievements were the work of just one man or woman. Jewish history is no different.

How impossible it is to fathom the far-reaching results of this one decision!

## GUARANTEED SUCCESS

An obvious question that follows what we have discussed is that the entire justification for the creation of man assumes that he actually follows through with the purpose of his creation—but is this always the case? What about the wicked? What about those who are just unaware of any such purpose in the first place?

Our Sages tell us in the Mishnah, "Every Jew has a share in the World to Come."[12] The reference to the World to Come in this passage applies specifically to the days of Mashiach, and in particular to the time of the resurrection of the dead.[13]

As explained, the time of Mashiach is when the ultimate objective in the creation of man—and the world at large—will be reached. The statement the Mishnah is making is that although there may be conditions and limits on the reward of the soul after it leaves the body, every Jew—body and soul together—will merit the time of the resurrection.

The reason for this is because, to quote another Talmudic passage, "Even the wicked among Israel are full of mitzvos as a pomegranate [is

---

11   *Koheles* 11:6.
12   *Mishnah Sanhedrin* 11:1.
13   The term *Olam Haba*, the World to Come, is used by our Sages both for the afterlife (when the soul is divested from the body) and to the time of the resurrection of the dead when the soul will be restored to the body in the physical world. The fact that the Mishnah here refers to the time of the resurrection is inferred from the context of this Mishnah. See *Bartenura; Midrash Shmuel* to *Sanhedrin* ibid.

full of seeds]."[14] The inclusion in the ultimate time of reward is due to the inevitable performance of many mitzvos by each Jew during their life here on earth. Mitzvos can only be performed while the soul is in the body. The ultimate reward for this will be upon the restoration of the soul to the body during the resurrection of the dead.

Although a person may have committed many wrongs, these wrong-doings are reversible, either by the person mending their ways in this world or with the cleansing process in the next world. This being the case, every Jew—regardless of their current state—must be looked upon as being "filled with mitzvos like a pomegranate." They are an indispensable part of the Divine plan and will ultimately be part of its fulfillment.

There is only one prerequisite for any of this to occur: that the soul descends to this earth to be vested in a physical body.

After the Mishnah states that "every Jew has a share in the World to Come," it goes on to enumerate several exceptions to this rule. These are examples of people who have done so much evil that they will not arise at the time of the resurrection.

What is important to note (and what other sources state) is that insofar as the *souls* of these individuals go, there is no such thing as a lost Jew. By whichever means, the soul will ultimately never be cast away and will merit a share in the World to Come by virtue of the mitzvos it inevitably performed. Once again, it must be underscored that this can only come to be if the soul is brought into the physical world in the first place.[15]

The third part of this book deals with the various practical issues that parents may think about when it comes to having another child. There

---

14   *Chagigah* 27a.
15   For a full treatise of this subject, see *To Live and Live Again*, Rabbi Nissan D. Dubov (New York: SIE, 1995), p. 43 ff. It is also worthy of noting that several sources indicate that even the *body* of such a Jew will eventually find its redemption as well. See *Talmud Yerushalmi Kilayim* 9:3; *Likutei Sichos* vol. 18, pp. 234–5 and footnotes there; ibid. pp. 409–10, footnote 71.

is one concern, however, that we will pick up on here, as it ties directly into the question above.

Parents are often concerned with whether they will successfully raise their children to follow the Torah way. While it goes without saying that parents must do all they possibly can to meet this goal, what must always remain clear is the unequivocal position of Torah that there is no such thing as a failed life. In fact, the only way for a life to fail, is for a life never to have been lived.

The above discussion pertains to those who could be held account-able for their actions. The question remains, however, regarding those individuals who were never given the opportunity in the first place to live a life devoted to Torah and mitzvos. This may be due to religious persecution, or, more prevalently, to a lack of Jewish education and/or positive exposure to it. If the purpose in creation is the study of Torah and the fulfillment of mitzvos, then how could we justify the high num-ber of Jews who are unable to answer this call, at no fault of their own?

If a person is given the opportunity and ability to perform a mitzvah, it is obvious that he must fulfill it. If they do not have the opportu-nity, then even with all the good intentions, the mitzvah has not been fulfilled. The exemption of the individual for the lack of opportunity does not render the mitzvah as having been performed. The lack is still there. How then can we justify the creation of man, given the practical inability to fulfill his purpose?

In truth, it is not within human capacity to know the thoughts of his Creator. Evidently though, there is a G-dly intention in putting Jews in such a situation.

Chassidic thought offers this idea: Sometimes, the anguish and bitterness that the person feels due to the lack of ability to perform a mitzvah brings forth the fact that the Jew is essentially and innately connected to G-d and will not find life satisfying without it. This yearn-ing and longing would never have come to be without the *inability* to perform the mitzvah. This is the concept of *teshuvah* that, as discussed above, is a large part of the objective behind the descent of the soul in the first place.

The above is but a glimpse into an arena that goes far beyond the comprehension of us mortals. What remains clear, though, is what the Talmud teaches: "The Holy One Blessed Be He does not deal imperiously (i.e., unreasonably) with His creatures."[16] Or, as the midrash puts it, "I [G-d] do not ask according to My strength but according to theirs."[17] If the purpose of an individual is to fulfill a certain mitzvah, then G-d will give them the opportunity to do so.

An important dimension to all the above pertains to those incapables of performing mitzvos due to bodily inability. This includes physical or mental handicap, illness, or a child passing at a young age, G-d forbid. No Jew (or human being) should ever have to endure such situations. In hindsight, however, there is a crucial purpose in the descent of each and every soul to this world. As stated, our understanding of this is limited indeed. Generally, though, our sources seem to identify such purpose in one of two ways:

- In a similar manner to the above, the mitzvos that such individuals *can* perform are the objective for their descent into this world. A well-known story is told of the Baal Shem Tov regarding a child that only lived until he was two years of age. The Baal Shem Tov comforted the parents by explaining that the soul of the boy had been of a very lofty caliber, and the only hindrance to its ascent in the Heavenly spheres was because as an infant it had nursed from a non-Jewish woman. The soul had come down to this world for this to be rectified, thus allowing for its total spiritual completion.
- There is purpose and effect in the mere presence of a Jew—body and soul—in this world. The mere existence of a Jew on this earth brings a G-dly presence into the world that internally elevates it.[18] Furthermore, the verse states: "The Heavens

16   *Avodah Zarah* 3a.

17   *Bamidbar Rabbah* 12:3.

18   See *Likutei Sichos* vol. 24, p. 163, footnote 43.

declare the glory of G-d."[19] In other words, the mere existence of creation brings out the glory of its Maker. By the same token, but to a far greater degree, the "praise of G-d" emerges from the mere existence of a Jew on earth.

One primary expression of this "praise" is in the eternity of the Jewish people. We are, as we have always been, a very small group, "the fewest among all nations."[20] Furthermore, the reality for the Jew has always been to be "as a sheep among seventy wolves." The volume of persecution and cruelty suffered by our people defies all comprehension. And yet we are here, while all the great ancient nations have been consigned to history. All this has been magnified manifold in modern times, with the generations of Jews living after the Holocaust. Indeed, a Jew living today is a living miracle. Just by living and walking this earth, the Jew is a testimony to the workings of G-d.[21]

Whether we fully understand it or not, the reality is that each Jew is an entire world. The Mishnah in which this phrase appears speaks of the stern warning given by a court to the witnesses in a case involving capital punishment.[22] The prohibition of murder applies to a child who is just a day old with the very same gravity as it applies to a grown adult. In contrast, on the positive side, the fact that each person is "an entire world" is not only due to their indispensable contribution by way of mitzvah performance, but, as demonstrated in the laws of life and death, a Jew is "an entire world" just by virtue of their existence in this world.

## CHIZKIYAHU'S MISTAKE

The Talmud tells the following story. Chizkiyahu, the righteous king of Judea, once became ill and the Almighty instructed the prophet Yeshayahu to go visit him. The verse tells us that the prophet was told by G-d to tell the king, "Thus says the L-rd of Hosts, 'Set your house

---

19   *Tehillim* 19:2.
20   *Devarim* 7:7.
21   For further elaboration on this concept, see *Sefer Hasichos* 5750, pp. 378–388.
22   *Mishnah Sanhedrin* 4:5.

in order, for you will die and you will not live.'"[23] The redundancy of stating "you will die" and "you will not live" referred to the fact that not only was the king not destined to live in this world, but that he had also lost his share in the World to Come.

Upon hearing this, Chizkiyahu was taken aback. "What is all of this?" he demanded to know. "What have I done wrong to deserve such a punishment?"

Yeshayahu told him that this was because the king had not "engaged in procreation"—Chizkiyahu had not married and had no children.

Chizkiyahu apologized and said, "I had no children because I envisaged, through Divine inspiration, that the children that would emerge from me will not be virtuous." As a result, Chizkiyahu thought it preferable to have no children at all.

Yeshayahu said to him, "Why do you involve yourself with the secrets of the Holy One Blessed Be He? That which you have been commanded [the mitzvah of procreation] you are required to perform, and that which is acceptable in the eyes of the Holy One Blessed Be He let Him perform."[24]

In the end, Chizkiyahu recovered and lived another fifteen years. He married Chefzibah, the daughter of Yeshayahu, and had two children. But Chizkiyahu's vision did in fact prove to be true. His son Menasheh grew up to be one of the most evil and corrupt kings in all of Jewish history. The verse attests to the fact that "Menasheh led Judah and the inhabitants of Jerusalem astray into evil even greater than that done by the nations that the L-rd had destroyed before the Israelites."[25] The actions of Menasheh and his generation were the cause for G-d's decision to eventually destroy Jerusalem and His Temple therein.[26]

Knowing this would happen was, seemingly, a strong case for Chizkiyahu to abstain from having children. Yet, he was condemned in the strongest of terms, and he ran the risk of losing both his physical and spiritual life as a result.

---

23  *Yeshayahu* 38:1.
24  *Berachos* 10a.
25  *Divrei Hayamim* II 33:9.
26  See *Melachim* II 21:23.

The commentaries on this passage of Talmud explain that although Chizkiyahu was correct in what he saw, he had nevertheless not seen the entire picture. Eventually, Menasheh did *teshuvah*.

The Book of *Divrei Hayamim* (Chronicles) records the event when the Assyrian army captured Menasheh and brought him in chains to Babylon.[27] In his distress, Menasheh "beseeched the L-rd his G-d, and he humbled himself greatly before the G-d of his fathers." G-d accepted his supplication and he later returned to Jerusalem a changed man. The verse records his efforts in mending some of the spiritual damage he had caused in the time prior to his repentance.

> *The Talmud Yerushalmi tells us that as the Babylonians were torturing him, Menasheh invoked the name of every deity in the world at the time, but to no avail. Seeing no way out, he finally said, "I remember that my father taught me the following verse while in the synagogue: 'When you are in distress and all these things have befallen you, at the end of days, you will return unto the L-rd, your G-d, and hearken to His voice. For the L-rd your G-d is a merciful G-d. He will not abandon you nor destroy you, and He will not forget the covenant of your forefathers that He swore to them.' I hereby call to Him," continued Menasheh, "if He answers me, good; but if not, then all of them are the same" [i.e., there is no difference between Him and the other deities who failed to help].*
>
> *The Talmud states that the ministering angels "sealed the windows of Heaven" so that the prayer of Menasheh could not be heard. The angels protested, "Master of the universe! This man who worshipped idols, who placed an idolatrous image in the Temple sanctuary—are you now going to accept his teshuvah?" The Almighty replied, "If I do not accept him, I will be closing the door on all others that wish to return."*
>
> *The Talmud concludes: "What did G-d do [now that the angels had 'sealed the windows of heaven']? He 'dug an*

---

27    Ibid., v. 10ff.

*opening under His throne of glory' and accepted Menasheh's supplication."*[28]

The Divine spirit that rested upon Chizkiyahu allowed him the knowledge of his son's sin, but not of his eventual return. Moreover, we read how the angels on high could not possibly fathom why G-d would accept *teshuvah* from such a man. They "sealed the windows of Heaven" and were successful in doing so.

Sin is a form of spiritual damage. The higher the level of G-dly consciousness, the more the spiritual damage of sin is felt. *Teshuvah* is a system of spiritual rectification, but, as in any limited setting, there are limitations to what can be rectified.

The Talmudic stories above bring us back to the beginning of our discussion. The angels on high failed to understand the relationship of G-d and the human being. Indeed, the entire human project is beyond the capacity of logic.

To the angels, the human project made no sense. The rationale was simple:

- That which is G-dly is good.
- That which is unG-dly is not.
- Man lives in a world of spiritual darkness in which not only does he not naturally feel G-dliness, but he can act in a way that is completely antithetical to it.

Yes, there can be righteous human beings, but the entire venture is fraught with danger, and many times it seems to be a proven failure. Why bother?

In another rather famous piece of Talmud, we find that when Moshe came to receive the Torah from G-d on Mount Sinai, the angles protested once again, "What is man that You are mindful of him and the son of man that You think of him... Place your majesty [the Torah] in the Heavens!"[29]

Rationally speaking, the creation of man indeed makes little sense. Its place is found in the unconventional and the supra-rational. It is the

---

28   *Talmud Yerushalmi Sanhedrin 52a.*
29   *Talmud Shabbos 88b.*

project of G-d in His deepest Self, the place in which the conventional or rational do not govern. This is *His* project.

The very fabric of man is a composition of two entirely different and contradictory elements: a physical body animated by a physical and animal-like soul, and a *neshamah*—a Divine and G-dly soul described as a "literal part of G-d."[30] The function of man is to effect the transformation of his body and the world around him into becoming a place for G-d Himself, something which, as discussed above, totally defies the rules of existence. This is again due to the infinite capacity given to man with which he can execute this project.

To achieve this, the soul must be clothed in, and united with, the physical body and world. If it were to remain a distant entity, merely being present in this world and not vested within it, it would not affect any genuine change. In order to elevate the world, the soul must be active within it, thus risking a situation of sin.

As described above, *teshuvah* is the expression of the inseparable bond of the soul to G-d. The process of *teshuvah* transforms the soul from having a finite bond with G-dliness to an infinite one. This is why, in the words of our Sages: "There is nothing that can stand in the way of *teshuvah*."[31]

Chizkiyahu's Divine vision allowed him to see beyond the constraints of time and place that are prevalent in the physical world. By such convention, however, the prospect of bearing an evil child did not look like a good idea. It was precisely for this that the prophet was told to rebuke him, saying, "Why do you involve yourself with the secrets of the Holy One Blessed Be He?" In other words, not only is your individual case a part of the "secrets of G-d" but the *entire human project* has no place from the vantage point you are speaking from. That is where the angels live, and they said not to create man in the first place. *The project of mankind begins where conventional reason ends.*[32]

---

30   See *Tanya*, chap. 2.
31   See *Rambam, Hilchos Teshuvah*, chap. 3.
32   See *Anaf Yosef; Ahavat Eitan; Chidushei Geonim* to *Ein Yaakov* on *Berachos* ibid.

It may be added that this idea is what is behind the tremendously harsh punishment that Yeshayahu foresaw—loss of life both in this world and in the World to Come—for the king. The lack of engagement in procreation portrayed a disengagement from the human project altogether. The punishment, therefore, can be viewed more as cause and effect: life in this world and life in the next are what characterize the project of mankind. By demonstrating his lack of identity with the human project, Chizkiyahu was, de facto, removing himself from these two worlds.

The Talmud tells us that "anyone who does not engage in procreation is as if he has 'spilled blood.'"[33] This comparison to murder is because the underpinning attitude of the two is essentially the same: murder defines an actual life as unimportant or unnecessary. The withholding of *potential* life is effectively a similar statement.

## NO PAIN, NO GAIN

Quoted above was the Talmudic passage whereby the Sages concluded that "better for man never to have been created." The Hebrew term that loosely translates in this context as "better" is *no'ach*. More accurately, however, the term actually describes a state of ease, rest, or comfort. "Better," or *no'ach*, is not a description of an objective good, but rather of a subjective one. This is precisely what the Sages meant with this passage:

It would have been a lot "easier," more "restful," more "comfortable," and subjectively much "better" for all parties concerned if man was not created…But there, in the essence of G-d Himself, is the fact that the very best can only be realized when this uneasy, unrestful, and uncomfortable being is created. No revelation or connection to G-d Himself can emerge from settling within the confines of convention. Indeed, it is only after the creation of man that G-d pronounces creation to be "*very* good."[34]

---

33   *Tosefta Yevamos*, chap. 8. *Shulchan Aruch Even Haezer* 1:1.
34   See *Likutei Torah Re'eh*, p. 28:4.

In the *Musaf* prayer of Yom Kippur, we echo the sentiment in this passage of Talmud by stating, "It was deliberated upon and decided in the council of Torah Sages: Happy is he who was not created." Here again, the key word is "happy" or in Hebrew, *ashrei*.[35]

This Hebrew term is used when describing a blissful, serene, and wonderful state of being. Most famously, this word is the first in a verse said three times a day in our prayers: "*Ashrei yoshvei veisecha*—Happy are those who dwell in your house."[36] It also appears as the first word in the book of *Tehillim*: "Happy is the man who has not walked in the counsel of the wicked, nor stood in the way of sinners, nor sat where scoffers sit. Rather, his desire is in the Torah of the L-rd; on his Torah he meditates day and night."

The intent of the statement in the Yom Kippur service is the same as the Talmudic passage from which it is taken. Not to have been created might have made for a much happier and blissful situation, but it would have simultaneously created the loss of the connection and revelation of G-d Himself that depends entirely on the work of man here on earth.

---

35  Some translate the word as it appears in the Yom Kippur service as "fortunate." However, this is inconsistent with the translation of the same word as it appears in other contexts, where it is translated as "happy."

36  *Tehillim* 84:5.

# CHAPTER 6

# *Purpose Achieved*

## A TREASURE

Our discussion until now was centered around an objective—the reward and greater purpose that is reached through the creation of man here on earth. In the final analysis, however, the most major statement of Judaism on this subject—the bomb, so to speak—tells us that having another child is not merely for the service of a greater purpose—great as it may be. The living Jew in this world is G-d's final and ultimate objective.

As explained above, the final purpose in creation is to be found in the fact that "G-d desired to dwell in the lowest of realms." A dwelling, in its perfect sense, is a place where the dweller can have a complete feeling of comfort and belonging. If there is a part in the dwelling that is a disturbance to the dweller, then the dwelling is incomplete. However, even once the dwelling is perfect and complete, it is still impossible to say that the person establishes a loving relationship with the bricks and mortar that make up his home...The structure of a home serves as the framework within which the truest sense of home can be realized: a life lived with those whom the person most deeply loves.

In a similar sense, the mission of the Jew is to make this world a home for G-d. To this end, every aspect of the world must be imbued with G-dliness. If there remains a part in the world that is not properly elevated, the job is incomplete. The elevation of the world, however, is only the framework within which the home for G-d, in its truest and innermost meaning, can be created. Now that the world is G-d's place, G-d can finally be with those to whom He is attached in the deepest possible way: the Jewish people.

The Torah describes the Jewish people as an *am segulah,* a treasured people to G-d."[1] Rashi interprets the Biblical term *segulah* as the kind of "costly vessels and precious stones that kings store away."

A close analysis of this description reveals that the kind of treasure the Torah speaks of here is of a very unique nature. There are treasures such as precious stones that are used to adorn the ornaments in a palace or even the royal crown itself. The purpose of these ornaments is to add honor and splendor to the king and his surroundings. But then there are treasures which are stored away from public eye; these do not add anything to the king's glory, for nobody can see them. Yet these are precisely the king's most treasured possessions.

All the other treasures that are on display are a means with which to further the king's honor and glory. This is a necessary part in the conduct of a king who must be held in high regard among his people. But then there are those treasures that are not on display. These are the items that touch the king on a deeply personal level. They are the treasures from which he derives content and pleasure privately, away from the public eye. They are not there to fulfill a certain function but are rather of intrinsic value, an end unto themselves.

The Jewish people are G-d's *segulah.* To G-d, the Jew is not merely the means through which His objective is fulfilled in this world; the Jew constitutes the objective itself. As it pertains to our discussion, the value of each additional child is not just because of their purpose and necessity, but ultimately because of their own infinite and intrinsic value to G-d Himself.

---

1    *Devarim* 14:2, 26:18.

It is vital to understand that when speaking of the Jew in this context, we are not merely referring to the Jewish soul. The intention is, in fact, predominantly to the Jewish *person*—body and soul together.

An oft-repeated theme throughout the Torah is that G-d chose the Jewish people from all other nations. To quote the verse above: "G-d has chosen you for Himself to be a treasured people from among all the peoples on the face of the earth."[2] Far from implying that the Jew is better than all the others, the idea of choice is specifically used in the description of this idea.

The term "choice" does not apply to a factual and existential bond. A parent does not choose a child; parent and child are one and inseparable from the onset. In the same sense, the soul is a G-dly being, completely and existentially connected to G-d in the deepest way possible. The relationship of the Jewish *soul* to G-d is characterized in this very manner: "You are *children* to Hashem your G-d."[3]

"Choice" implies a situation where there is no automatic attachment to a certain item. G-d choosing the Jewish people is not a reference to the Jewish soul; it refers to the Jewish body.

The significance of G-d's attachment to the Jewish body is great indeed.

The fact that a parent is bound with a child is a rule—a rule of physical and spiritual nature. Moreover, this is a rule in the G-dly sphere as well: the Jewish soul is a child to G-d. If, however, we are to enter a situation where no rules and conventions apply, then this bond too can be put to the question. Although the bond between G-d and the soul is factual and existential, this still does not speak about G-d Himself, Who is above all facts and rules.

Conversely, the nature of the body is the complete opposite of the soul. The soul is G-dly, it expresses and exudes G-dliness. The body, on the other hand expresses only itself, not G-dliness. In other words, by every standard of facts and rules, the body is no G-dly thing.

Saying that G-d chose, i.e. attached, Himself to the body means that we are speaking of an attachment that comes from a place which

---

2    *Devarim* 14:2.
3    Ibid., 14:1; *Tanya*, chap. 2.

is beyond facts, rules, and givens. This is from Him. In fact, it is this attachment to the Jewish person—body and soul together—that elevates the *soul* to an entirely higher and deeper bond with G-d.[4]

This attachment, or choice, in the physical Jew finds expression in the boundless love that G-d has for the Jew here on earth. As we state in the holiday *Amidah* prayer: "You have chosen us from all the nations. You have loved us…" Or, as we say each day in the blessing before the *Shema*: "You have chosen us from among all nations and tongues, and you, our King, have lovingly brought us close to Your great Name."

Rav Shneur Zalman of Liadi, the first Rebbe of Chabad, would say, "We have absolutely no conception how precious to G-d is the body of a Jew."

This fact is what is behind the idea that the ultimate destiny in the days of Mashiach will not be for the soul as it is divested from the body, but rather in the union of body and soul in this world (hence the resurrection of the dead in time to come). The Jewish soul, as lofty as it is, is not the ultimate. The physical Jew here on earth is where it's all at.[5]

## THE GREATEST PRIVILEGE

The import of all of the above is that the birth of an additional child is the greatest gift and the highest privilege that G-d can bestow on a married couple. The nearest and dearest thing to G-d is the physically living Jew here on earth. It is this priceless gift that G-d entrusts to a Jewish mother and father. Every additional child endlessly magnifies this incredible privilege.

A story is told of a mother who was walking up a steep hill as she was carrying her child. A passerby commented that the child must be burdensome for her. The mother responded, "This is not a burden, this is a child."

Viewing a child, and for that matter an adult, in this way adds a crucial dimension to this discussion. The love of G-d for the Jew is intrinsic:

---

4    *Tanya*, chap. 49. See *Toras Shalom*, p. 120 ff.
5    *Likutei Sichos*, vol. 24, pp. 162–4; vol. 15, p. 384 (and footnote 18 ad loc.); vol. 17, p. 222.

to G-d, the physical Jew is the arrival at the final goal and purpose. As explained, this is not just in reference to the Jewish soul, but in the most major way—to the Jewish body. The application of this has incredible bearing on the approach of parents to the care they provide for their children: The various tasks involved in raising a family must be viewed as sacred and intrinsically holy activities, *in and unto themselves.* As understood from the above, this not only applies to spiritual care, but, in a most major way, to the physical care for bodily needs.

## HANDS OFF

The attitude above, which must be directed toward any Jew, is additionally magnified with the unique specialty of Jewish children. One of the many ways in which our Sages express this is the following: Speaking in the name of G-d, the prophet states: "Do not touch My anointed ones."[6] The Talmud explains that the term "My anointed ones" refers to Jewish children."[7] The Hebrew term of Mashiach, the Messiah, actually also means "the anointed one." The way that kings were appointed in Judaism was by being anointed with oil. Mashiach, who will be the king appointed by G-d, is therefore referred to in this way. Giving each Jewish child the title of Mashiach means that there is a direct correlation and connection between the two.

The teachings of Kabbalah explain that Mashiach will embody the deepest faculty of the soul, known as the *yechidah*. This will enable Mashiach to bring the world and mankind to express the deepest point of their own existence, and in turn connect them to the deepest and truest self of G-d.

Although the *yechidah* is powerfully existent within each Jew, it usually does not play an active role in daily life. Above our deepest and truest self is an entire gamut of faculties and abilities which govern our regular consciousness. For better or worse, our intellect and everyday emotions conceal our innermost selves. Spiritually, our connection

---

6    *Divrei Hayamim* I 16:22.
7    *Shabbos* 119b.

with the Divine operates in a similar way. The connection that exists within the recesses of the soul is, for the most part, hidden.

The thing about children, though, is that their faculties are not fully developed. Physically, it is in children where we can see the intuitive and core nature of the human being, in a way that is far less conditioned and manipulated than in an adult. Spiritually, it is the same. Precisely due to the lack of developed spiritual faculties in a child, the pure and simple connection with G-d is apparent. Young children do not know of sophistication and complication, and it is precisely this which allows their factual and essential connection with G-d to be visible.

This is the meaning behind the description of Mashiach that the verse gives to each Jewish child: like Mashiach, each Jewish child personifies the revelation of the essential connection to G-d, embodied by the deepest level of the soul—the *yechidah*.

This quality within a child is reflected in another Talmudic passage: "The world only endures because of the 'breath' (Torah recitation) of schoolchildren."[8] This statement is not even said with regard to the greatest Sages, for as the Talmud itself explains: "The breath of adults, which is tainted by sin, cannot be compared to the breath of children, which is not tainted by sin."

The innocence and purity of a Jewish child connects directly to G-d. The gift and privilege of having another child is only magnified by the intense specialty of G-d's relationship specifically with small children.

## ANOTHER JEWISH CHILD

Our analysis so far has been of the ideas as they exist on the fundamental and cosmic level. In closing, though, there is more to be said, and it is by no means detached from everything discussed above. The tone here does change, however, as the following often belongs to the realm of emotion.

The upheavals of the last century have seen tragedies and triumphs unparalleled in our long history. Living in a time like ours obligates

---

8    Ibid.

every Jew to contemplate these extraordinary events and draw the appropriate conclusions.

The devastation and unimaginable suffering of our people must be ever-present in the consciousness of a Jew. The events of the Holocaust and the related horrors, both before and after, must stir the soul to no end. Merely identifying, however strongly, with the story of our people is very far from sufficient. These events must first and foremost invoke action.

In reference to the suffering of the Jews in Egypt the Torah states that "as much as they would afflict them, so they would increase and so they would spread out."[9] In the wake of witnessing such evil, the Jewish resolve must be to build and celebrate precisely that which the enemy sought to destroy. The ultimate response to the attempt of obliterating the Jew is the creation of another Jewish life. There can be no greater blow to the Jew haters of both past and present than the birth of another precious Jewish child. It is the greatest statement for the triumph of light over darkness, of life over all that opposes it.

An incredible display of how the sanctity and value of childbirth were so ingrained in the Jewish psyche was seen in the months and years immediately following the Holocaust. The Displaced Persons (DP) camps were the temporary refuge for many survivors who had lost everything to the Nazi ravage and had been subject to years of unspeakable horror.

Ada Schein, a researcher on the DP camps, gives us some description:

> *The enormity of the social and emotional devastation of the concentration camp survivors was so great that not even the joy of liberation could temper it. Reports by the liberating forces and the testimony of survivors reveal passivity, apathy, a profound sense of alienation, estrangement, hostility, social anxiety, unhappiness, and a burden of loneliness accompanied by fear of the future. Many suffered from impaired memory, inability to concentrate, restlessness, fits of rage, weeping for no apparent reason as a result of emotional anxiety, hypersensitivity, and a low response threshold. Upon liberation, the*

---

9    *Shemos* 1:12.

*women, like the men, suffered from severe infectious diseases and from tuberculosis.*

*With the restoration of the family unit starting in the summer of 1945, there slowly began to emerge signs of a social transformation in the lives of the survivors. Data from the camp at Bergen-Belsen indicate that during 1946, 1,070 marriages took place in this camp alone; the first year following liberation saw six to seven weddings a day, and sometimes even fifty in one week.*

*...The women devoted the bulk of their energy to bearing children and raising a family. The fear that their fertility had been impaired pushed many women to become pregnant even before they had healed from the ongoing damage of privation and disease. Pregnancies and births took place in the DP camps in such unprecedented numbers that researchers have referred to the phenomenon as a "baby boom." There are those who see the high birth rate as a form of revenge against the death and destruction caused by the war.*

*Data from the American-occupied zone in Germany indicate a striking rise in the population of infants and children under five during 1946. In January 1946, there were 120 children under the age of five; by September of that year, the number had reached 4,430. According to a report by the American Jewish Joint Distribution Committee (known as the Joint) in late November 1946, out of 134,541 Jewish displaced persons in the American zone, 3.2 percent were infants of up to one year, 3.5 percent were children aged between one and five, and 10.5 percent were children from the ages of six to fifteen. In 1947, the birth rate in the DP camps reached 50.2 per thousand, one of the highest in the world.[10]*

As we turn our attention to the present, there can be no mistake that the magnificent renaissance of the Jewish people in the last half

---

10    Ada Schein, "She'erit ha-Peletah: Women in DP Camps in Germany," in *Jewish Women: A Comprehensive Historical Encyclopedia*, March 1, 2009, Jewish Women's Archive.

century is rivaled only by the intensity of devastation witnessed just before it. Any Jew with some sense of history and peoplehood must be filled today with a deep sense of exhilaration and intense pride. True, there are great problems. But little can parallel the magnitude of Jewish revival witnessed in our time.

In no era in history—even very recent history—have Jews across the globe been so free and unrestricted from living fully Jewish lives. Our age has brought with it the accessibility and ease of Torah study and mitzvah performance in a fashion that our ancestors could have only dreamed of. This is true even in the diaspora, to say nothing of the Divine, historic, and breathtaking miracle that has taken place in our day: the return to the Land of Israel.

We, the eternal people of G-d, have once again emerged victorious, and what a victory it is. *Am Yisrael Chai.*

The large, robust, and life-filled Jewish family is a celebration of the Jewish people and Jewish life. Bringing another Jewish child into the world is the expression of joy and thanks for a living G-d, an eternal Torah, a life of meaning and holiness; for the Land of Israel; and for the great days of an imminent redemption.

Each additional child strengthens the Jewish people in the most literal way. Aside from strength in numbers, a child raised as a Jew will no doubt be able to carry our sacred tradition, not only for themselves, but to bear the torch and illuminate the lives of others as well.

Every child born today will be born into the era that stands on the threshold of Mashiach's coming. As the world around us changes at unimaginable speed, we are living witnesses to the most intense and unprecedented era in history. The children born today will be of the last in the arduous exile, and, we hope very soon, to be among those to behold the ultimate redemption.

PART 2

# Benefits

*In its encouragement of keeping the mitzvos, the Torah emphasizes that these commandments are "for your good" (Devarim 10:13). The continuity of having children brings tremendous blessing in many tangible and immediate ways. In the following pages, we will explore some aspects of the great good an additional child can bring along.*

# CHAPTER 7

# The Greatest Joy

## INTRODUCTION

Although we live differently today than in previous centuries, not all change is progress. Our current Western culture idolizes the "I," the self. From self-actualization and self-help to self-confidence and self-esteem, we all live in this culture and know it well. Reality, however, has proven the truth that Judaism has always known: inner fulfillment and true joy come precisely and exclusively from living up to that which is higher, and other, than the self.

Viewed as they should be, children are a true and endless source of joy, and the work associated with them are a labor of love. The joy and gratification experienced in seeing children live, grow, and flourish is unmatched.

Each child is unique in his or her own way. The joy and satisfaction emanating from one child will never be the same as that from another. This variation will eventually also be part of the endless delight for the parents and family at large.

A little knowledge of Jewish history and some level of imaginative skill will allow the modern Jew to picture the atmosphere in a Jewish family before the age of family planning set in. True, there were hardships, and at times even extreme challenges. But how much genuine warmth and light poured forth from the Jewish home—with the primary source being the multiple children and the *nachas* emanating from them. Thankfully, there are so many wonderful examples of such families today.

Human nature is that "he who possesses one hundred wants two hundred."[1] The enjoyment derived from the children already born into a family should certainly bring a desire to have another.

An additional dimension to this is the cumulative joy simply coming about from the many occasions and *simchahs* celebrated in a large family. The circumcisions, baby namings, first haircuts (*upsherin*), bar/bas mitzvahs, weddings, birthdays, educational milestones, and anniversaries—all these are opportunities for celebration and good cheer. This becomes increasingly valuable later in life. As children marry and have children of their own, the increase in joyous occasions can equal or even override the sadder events, if only on a quantitative level.

## FUTURE INVESTMENT

"All beginnings are difficult," say our Sages.[2] Many benefits of additional children come later in life.

Children eventually grow older, leave their parents' home, and go about building their own lives. Parents with fewer children often experience what is termed today as "empty nest syndrome," the loneliness parents feel after children come of age and leave their childhood homes.

The joy of grandparenthood is usually not accompanied with the same degree of responsibility that parents have. Grandchildren, or even great-grandchildren, can be a pure and endless source of happiness and pleasure to their grandparent—and vice versa. With fewer children, these joys will necessarily be capped. Grandparents cannot constantly be present in the homes and lives of their grandchildren, as privacy and

---

1    See *Koheles Rabbah* 1:13 and 3:10.
2    *Mechiltah Shemos* 19:5.

space for the parents—their children—must be maintained. In these years, both parents and children are generally busy, and do not have ample time to spend with their grandparents. All this is especially true if the children move further away from their parents' home.

In a larger family, the excitement and color of family life rarely wanes. The constant stream of calls, visits, and get-togethers allows grandparents the *nachas* and joy that only family life can bring.

The returns derived from additional children applies powerfully in the spiritual arena as well. Bringing children into the world not only offers them the possibility of living a lifetime of mitzvos; it also creates the possibility for them to have children of their own who will be able to do the same. The multiplied blessing of one child will continue to increase with each generation.

In truth, there is no way of measuring the value of one single mitzvah, let alone a lifetime filled with them. A mitzvah is a connection to G-d, and even just one mitzvah is something infinite and ultimate. As parents gaze at the horizon of a potential child, the mere knowledge of setting into motion a lifetime to be filled with literally millions of mitzvos is magnificent indeed. The causal effect of future lives that this life will bring forth gives the above infinite magnitude.

Aside from the incredible value of this on a conceptual level, there is additional dimension of benefit in this for the parents themselves. Our Sages state that the good deeds of children bring merit and blessing to their parents both in this world and in the next. It is for this reason that children are encouraged and even obligated to study Torah and perform mitzvos in honor of their deceased parents. Our Sages teach that righteous deeds of children cause a tremendous degree of spiritual elevation for the soul of the parent.[3] An additional child only multiplies such spiritual benefit.

---

3    See *Ohr Zarua*, vol. 2, chap. 50.

## JEWISH STRENGTH AND CONTINUITY

One of lowest points in Jewish history was during the destruction of the Second Temple and the aftermath of Roman oppression. In one gripping passage, the Talmud relates the following:

> *Rabbi Yishmael ben Elisha said:…From the day that the [Roman] government put upon us evil decrees, prohibiting to us the Torah and its commandments, not allowing us to circumcise and redeem our children, it would be only right that we should take upon ourselves not to marry and have children, and in that way, the descendants of Avraham would be destroyed by themselves…but leave Israel alone, let them do as they please, as it is better they should sin unintentionally than intentionally (i.e., if such conduct should be ordered, the people would certainly not observe it).[4]*

Some of the commentaries on the Talmud clarify that this was more a statement of grief than a practical contemplation. There was no actual consideration of decreeing against marriage and childbirth; it was rather the intensity of persecution that found expression in these agonizing words.[5] The commentary of the *Tosafos*, however, seems to take Rabbi Yishmael's remarks literally. The *Tosafos* is obviously taken aback:

> *This is a wonder! Does the Torah not mandate, "Be fruitful and multiply?" It may be suggested that this passage refers to those who have already fulfilled the obligation to "be fruitful and multiply" [by having a son and a daughter]. What is meant by the statement 'so that the children of Avraham would be destroyed by themselves' is that Jews would only have one son and daughter.*

It is interesting that the *Tosafos* does not offer any evidence for this assumption as it does for many of its arguments. To be sure, however,

---

4    *Bava Basra* 60b.
5    *She'eilos U'Teshuvos Beis Yosef* 14.

there was no need to. Living with cognizance of Jewish history, including the era in which the authors of *Tosafos* themselves lived, made this comment self-understood: *Having only the minimal number of children would guarantee the extinction of the Jewish people.*

The Torah insists on the fact that Jews are responsible for one another. We are one family. Every Jewish couple plays an integral part in creating the future of the Jewish people. Never again should our people experience the kind of horrific events we endured in our long history. In hindsight, however, there were many generations of Jews who could have decided to collectively have fewer children. They didn't, and that is why we are here today.

Aside for guaranteeing the very continuity of the Jewish people, it is certain that each additional Jewish child will strengthen and fortify Jewish life, the Land of Israel, and everything that we hold holy and dear.

The truth in this idea was powerfully proven in our most recent history. After the devastation of the Holocaust and communist Russia, it can be said, with certainty, that the unprecedented renaissance of Jewish life today is significantly due to the devotion and commitment of Jewish men and women to having large families.

## THE CASE FOR SIBLINGS

Modern day research confirms a series of multilevel benefits associated with children who have siblings. In many of the examples cited below, an increased number of siblings also increases the level of benefit they can bring.[6]

### Health Benefits

Studies have demonstrated that younger siblings enjoy substantial protection against allergies like eczema and hay fever, as well as a host

---

6    The researched material in the following paragraphs has largely come from the work of Colin Brazier and Therese Walin in their book, *Sticking up for Siblings: Who's Deciding the Size of Britain's Families?* (Civitas, 2013).

of other autoimmune and more serious conditions. In the case of hay fever, incidents were seen to be more than halved if a child had two or more siblings. Similar findings applied to eczema.[7]

In 2011, after examining the records of 13,000 children ages five to seven, a team of Japanese researchers discovered that while the prevalence of food allergies was 4 percent for the eldest or sole child, it fell to 3.5 percent for the second, and fell further to 2.6 percent for those born after. In other words, the risk of a potentially serious food allergy was found to be almost halved for a third child.[8]

To date, although several theories have been offered, there seems to be no conclusive medical explanation as to why all of this is the case. The "hygiene hypothesis" has been one of the more influential attempts, claiming that exposure in early life to bacteria and viruses has influence on the development of the immune system. Swapping germs at an early age with siblings does just this, which in turn causes their immune systems to better develop. What remains interesting though is that daycare and nursery attendance, also a known arena for germ swapping, does not seem to produce similar results, or at least it seems to do so only for very young children.

Other hypotheses have credited these child immunities to changes in the mother's immune system caused by multiple pregnancies. Regardless of explanation, however, the factual statistical findings are well-established and substantial.

Another major area of sibling advantage is decrease in obesity. Many studies have confirmed that risk of obesity is much greater for a child without any siblings, while at least one major study found that the odds for obesity decrease by fourteen percent for each additional sibling in the household.[9]

---

7   D.P. Strachan, "Hay Fever, Hygiene, and Household Size," BMJ 1989;299:1259, https://www.bmj.com/content/299/6710/1259.

8   See Jennifer Warner, "Birth Order May Affect Risk of Allergies," Webmd.com, March 21, 2011, https://www.webmd.com/allergies/news/20110321/birth-order-may-affect-risk-of-allergies.

9   S. Kimm and N. Glynn, "The Role of Sociodemographic, Physiologic and Behavioral Predictors of Weight Outcomes, Dietary Behaviors, and Physical Activity," University of Pittsburgh, 2004.

Here again there seems to be a lack of sufficient scientific discourse for the explanation of this phenomenon. Anecdotally, it is clear that siblings initiate a great amount of action and play between themselves, thus allowing for many unwanted calories to be burned in the process.

## Skills, Development, and Character

Being part of a larger family contributes in many positive ways to the personality of a child. To begin with, children of larger families are pushed in their development in a multitude of areas by both their younger and older siblings. Furthermore, the atmosphere and culture in a larger family will usually nurture some incredibly valuable life skills and character traits in children.

Some common examples:

- Responsibility and capability: Larger families bring with them multiplied household chores and responsibilities. Children learn that they need to do their part, and as time goes by, they get good at it. Among other responsibilities, this includes the ability of care, as older siblings often care for younger ones.
- Independence: In a large family, children come to understand that not everything can be done for them all the time. Children in such families pick up more quickly how to do things on their own.
- Gratification deferment: Having to wait your turn is great training.
- A reduced sense of entitlement: Children are happy with—and enjoy—the smaller things in life. Constantly having to share with siblings imbues children with the fact that sharing with others is integral to life itself.
- Social and interpersonal skills: The constant interaction with siblings hones an entire gamut of social and interpersonal skills within children. Some of these include conflict resolution, anger management, getting along with people who are different, empathy, comfort, helping others, respect for another's property, and dealing with pressure. Once again, aside from being

anecdotally true, the above has also been established by several major and relatively recent studies.[10]

## Social Capital

Siblings can be an invaluable source of support to each other in so many ways. The more siblings there are, the more variety and availability for such support. An individual sibling will be able to turn to multiple sources of sibling support, or to the specific sibling they feel is best at the given situation.

With friends, however dear, there will usually be some element of formality and inability for total openness. Siblings are able to speak and act in a more primal, and possibly honest, manner.

Siblings are points of reference throughout the entirety of life. Coworkers, friends, and even parents cannot be counted on for being present at all stages of life. Siblings often are, especially if there are many.

The closeness and understanding of siblings is strong and acute. In adult life, this too can be of great advantage. To quote the author of *Sticking up for Siblings:*

> In a world where it is ever easier to reinvent and make over ourselves, siblings hold us to account. Over the course of the entire lifespan nobody stands a better chance of highlighting our contradiction and identifying our hypocrisies than our own siblings. Where introspection fails, siblings stand a good chance of being the true custodians of conscience.[11]

One significant benefit of multiple siblings is when it comes to caring for aging parents or grandparents. Although in many cases, one or several of the siblings will take the bulk of responsibility, it is nevertheless incomparable when there are multiple brothers and sisters who can

---

10 See for example: D.B. Downey and D.J. Condron, "Playing Well with Others in Kindergarten: The Benefit of Siblings at Home," *Journal of Marriage and Family* 66(2):333-350, 2004, https://psycnet.apa.org/record/2004-15844-007; and Amelia Hill, "Sibling Rivalry 'Good for Children,'" *The Guardian*, April 7, 2011.

11 P. 40.

contribute in their own way. This makes things far easier and more doable both for the primary caregivers and for everyone else concerned.

On the joyous side, siblings will form a treasure chest of resource and assistance when it comes to occasions of family celebration, not to mention the joy they will most certainly add to the *simchah* itself.

PART 3

# *Practicalities*

Until now, we have sought to establish the principled Torah approach
to the birth of an additional child as well as some of the great benefits
associated with this decision. At this point, we will venture into
addressing some of the practical concerns attached to this.
Perhaps the most important idea to bear in mind is the fact that
hundreds of thousands of Jewish families in the modern age have
successfully raised many children to be everything a parent could
possibly desire. Although this takes a high level of commitment, the
project has proven to be both doable and incredibly fulfilling. The
approach to the various practicalities discussed below have been put
to the test countless times in multiple situations.

CHAPTER 8

# Finances

## COMFORT OR NECESSITY?

Finances are often cited as the greatest consideration for limiting family size. The concern will usually take on one of two forms:

- Additional children may consume the bulk of financial resources, thus limiting expenditure on otherwise affordable comforts.
- The current level of family income cannot seem to sustain additional children.

As the two concerns are obviously quite different from one another, a unique Torah perspective is necessary to address each of them.

## JEWISH RICHES

The subject we will first address is that of additional comforts or luxuries, which may become less affordable when choosing to have another child.

To begin, it must be underscored that from a Torah perspective, it is imperative that we serve G-d with "joy and gladness of the heart."[1] In

---

1    *Devarim* 28:47; *Rambam Hilchos Lulav* 8:15; *Shelah, Yud Maamaros, maamar* 3, 4 (49a).

this way, the various pleasures of life can and should be enjoyed. The subject of this discussion is not about those things necessary for this state of everyday contentment. It rather pertains to those pleasures which a person can do well without: luxuries.

We must be candid about the fact that the truly worthwhile things in life demand some level of sacrifice. There are no real exceptions to this rule. This question therefore becomes one of priority. It must be internalized that what is at stake here is the entire life of a person, a Jew, a child, with all the colossal meaning and significance this carries.

Our short time in this world should be utilized wisely. The opportunity for achieving something of infinite, G-dly value should be embraced with joy and gratitude.

Our tradition is replete with analogies, parables, and anecdotes that bring out this point. One such parable is of a devoted servant who was given just one hour by the king to collect as many royal treasures as he could. As he was brought to the royal treasury, the most enchanting music began to be played before him. The unfortunate servant spent the entire hour listening to the pleasurable music, and after the hour was over, he emerged empty-handed. A similar story is told of the man who was washed up on an island strewn with gold and diamonds, but the island's currency was onions. He collected ship loads of the island's valuable currency only to return home and realize how terribly shortsighted he had been.

The magnitude of value and centrality in the choice of having another child would have been sufficient even if no physical or material benefit were to accompany it. As we have explained, however, there are so many aspects of tremendous benefit and genuine satisfaction gained by having additional children.

Humanity is witness to the fact that wealth and material affluence do not create happiness and fulfillment in the long run.[2] An additional child, in many more ways than one, can bring an increase of true joy and fulfillment to his or her parents.

---

2    Several recent studies continue to confirm this concept. See for example: Arthur C. Brooks, "A Formula for Happiness." *The New York Times*. Dec. 14, 2013. J. Hale, "What Makes Us Happy?" *Psych Central*. (2016).

In closing, it is worthy of noting that the pursuit of material luxuries and pleasures is generally frowned upon in Jewish thought. The Torah enjoins us in many places to "be holy." Our Sages understand this as an instruction to "sanctify yourself in that which is permitted to you." The pursuit and submergence in materialism for its own sake distracts and desensitizes a person from spirituality and G-dliness. [3]

## BORN WITH A LOAF IN HAND

The second form of financial concern is expressed when the current level of family income does not seem to sustain additional children.

Properly addressing this from a Jewish perspective necessitates the introduction of two fundamental Torah ideas.

- "The One Who gives life gives sustenance."[4] When G-d gives someone a child, He gives along with it the means of its support.
- "And G-d will bless you in all that you do."[5] G-d's blessing comes through the efforts of man.

The first principle is laid down by the Torah in multiple places. The verse in *Tehillim* states that G-d "gives nourishment to all flesh, for His kindness endures forever."[6] The opening part of the *Birkas Hamazon* (Grace after Meals) is entirely devoted to the fact that G-d "prepares nourishment for all the creations that He created." "A child is born," says the Talmud, "with his loaf [i.e., sustenance] in hand."[7]

This idea provides basis for the fact that having additional children is different than many other mitzvah endeavors. In most cases, we are instructed not to overspend beyond our means even for a holy cause.[8] Having an additional child, however, is entirely different: With the birth of each child, their parents are simultaneously creating the avenue of their sustenance. This sustenance is automatically granted and

---

3    See *Ramban, Vayikra* 20:7.
4    A phrase based upon *Taanis* 8b.
5    *Devarim* 15:18.
6    *Tehillim* 136:25.
7    *Niddah* 31b.
8    See for example, *Shabbos* 133b. *Shulchan Aruch Yoreh Deah* 249:1.

available. It is the privilege and merit of parents to pass this blessing on to their children for the time that the Almighty has entrusted them to do so.

The degree to which this blessing extends is also important to understand. The Almighty does not expect a Jew to have many children and live on a substandard economic level as a result. The very same Torah that encourages the birth of additional children also instructs the Jew to do what is necessary in maintaining a respectable socio-economic standard of living.[9] The Talmud also states that, within reason, a person is obligated to provide for his wife and children (somewhat) beyond his own economic ability.[10]

Although there are endless variations as to what might characterize a mainstream respectful lifestyle, the general rule is that a person should judge his expenditures by assessing a genuine need, along with evaluating what is commonly accepted in his culture and community.

If finances are raised as a concern for having an additional child, the first objective is to arrive at an honest and truthful analysis of current family expenditure. It may be time for some soul searching and restructuring. Often after contemplation with oneself, one's spouse, or a trusted friend or mentor, a very different picture emerges.

Sometimes, such assessments can eliminate the concern. If this is not the case, an additional set of questions must be asked.

## AND G-D WILL BLESS YOU IN ALL THAT YOU DO

Although G-d "gives bread to all flesh," the "bread" is generally not given without an adequate measure of effort on the part of the recipient. This is true of "all flesh," but especially so with regard to man. From the first moment of his creation on earth, the Almighty conveyed to Adam that

---

9    See *Rambam, Hilchos Deos* 1:5; *Shulchan Aruch Orach Chaim* 156:1. This is reflected in the text of the *Kesubah* which states the commitment of the husband to "work, honor, feed and support you [the wife] in the custom of Jewish men, who work, honor, feed, and support their wives faithfully."

10   *Chullin* 84b; *Rambam,* ibid.

his mission would be to "work it."[11] "Man is born to toil," says the verse.[12] Earning a living is usually the primary fulfillment of these dictums.

In many places, our Sages underscore the imperative of hard work. "Love work!" urges the Mishnah.[13] "Skin a carcass in the market and take payment, but do not say, 'I am a great man and this matter is beneath me.'"[14]

An integral aspect to the above is that the effort invested in one's work must be commensurate with the yield that is necessary to come from it. In our case, settling for a very low-paying or part-time job can hardly be considered making the adequate "vessel" for the sustenance of a larger family. A person needs to be responsible.

It is interesting that the two ideas—enjoying the "labor of one's hands" and having a large family—are blessings that Scripture juxtaposes one to another:

> *When you eat the labor of your hand, you are praiseworthy, and it is well with you. Your wife will be like a fruitful vine in the inner chambers of your home; your children will be like olive shoots surrounding your table. Behold, for so is blessed a man who fears G-d.*[15]

If after an honest analysis there is still a question as to whether a current income can sustain another child, the next stage would be an examination of whether one is investing a sufficient level of effort in creating the necessary amount of income.

Once again, aside for the obvious teamwork with one's spouse, it is often helpful to discuss these matters with friends, a mentor, or even a professional coach. Are there other possible sources of revenue? Maybe an additional side job? A change of career or location? A request for a raise? All viable options should be explored.

---

11    *Bereishis* 2:15.
12    *Iyov* 5:7.
13    *Avos* 1:10.
14    *Bava Basra* 110a.
15    *Tehillim* 128:2–5.

Sometimes income can be increased, and sometimes expenses can be decreased. The obvious objective is to reach the point where income and expense either meet or come reasonably close.

## TUITION COSTS

Within the realm of financial concerns for the Jewish family today, little can compare to the concern of tuition payments for day school and higher Jewish education. Jewish children belong in a Jewish school, and tuition can be expensive.

It is no secret that currently, the cost of tuition is one of the strongest reasons Jewish parents consider limiting their family size. The intensity of the issue differs somewhat from one place to another, usually depending on the extent that a local government will subsidize Jewish schooling. In general, though, Jewish education is not cheap. Our discussion would be incomplete without addressing this burning issue.

In the realm of Jewish education, we currently live both in the best and the worst of times.

On the one hand, we are living through a wonderful and unprecedented age of Jewish history. Never, in three and a half thousand years, has it ever been possible for every Jewish child, male and female, to receive a full elementary and higher Jewish education. On the other hand, the reality is that in today's day and age, giving each child a Jewish education is not a nicety or a luxury—it is an absolute necessity.

In previous centuries, if a child did not receive a full Jewish education, there could still be reasonable expectation for them to grow and live as committed Jews. This was certainly true of girls who until modern times, often had no formal Jewish education at all. Children grew up and remained true to their Judaism by virtue of expectation and inspiration from their home and environment. This is not to say that the project was always successful, but for much of our history, there was no major reason to suspect that this system would fail. Today, the reality has radically changed. The sadly proven fact is that failure to provide a child and teenager with proper Jewish schooling is putting their entire Jewish identity at risk, not to speak of their

Torah observance. This is true for the child, and far more so, for their children and grandchildren.[16]

In a similar way to the overall family planning issue, the current dynamics of Jewish education have never been experienced before. Once again, a situation like this requires us to look back into the Torah and draw guidance from our endless source of G-dly wisdom.

It is important to note that although the primary responsibility for Torah education lies with the individual parent, the concept of universal Jewish schooling was created with the understanding that in practicality, it would require help from the wider community. The application of this took on various forms in various places and times, but regardless of method, it was the community at large that was obligated to ensure a basic Jewish education for every Jewish child.[17]

In other words, there was never any expectation that every Jewish family would be able to afford the necessary means for their children to study Torah. It was self-understood that Torah education for every child was a *collective* project, not an individual one.

Now, all of the above was true at a time when just an elementary Torah education for boys was seen to suffice. Today, the consensus across the Torah-observant Jewish world is that such a level of education is far from sufficient. In our time, the necessity is not only for every young child, male or female, to be in a Jewish school environment, but for every young adult as well. There is no alternative. It is clear that the general Jewish community, or the more affluent members of it, now carry a much different and far greater level of responsibility.

For better or for worse, the collective responsibility for Torah education today has become the task either of the institutions themselves,

---

16 Several studies have established the profound impact of Jewish day school attendance or lack thereof on adult Jewish identity. See S.M. Cohen and L. Kotler-Berkowitz, "The Impact of Childhood Jewish Education upon Adults' Jewish Identity." Jewish Community Report Series on the National Jewish Publication Survey 2000-2001, July 2004.

17 See *Shulchan Aruch HaRav, Hilchos Talmud Torah* 1:3–4.

or of the umbrella organization they are part of. Budgets are usually covered by a combination of government funding, communal fundraising efforts, and tuition paid by parents. Halachah dictates that the amount of tuition paid by parents should be based on the capability of the family.[18] One major contributing factor is family size.

If it is to remain true to its Torah values, a Jewish educational institution must take family size into account when assessing the means of the parents to meet tuition costs. More affluent members of a community should understand that it is their halachic duty to give more than the actual cost of their own children's education in order to cover for those less capable of doing so.[19]

Insofar as our discussion is concerned, the fact remains that the parents still carry the primary responsibility to provide a Jewish education for their children; community responsibility is merely a backup. But if the need so arises, a parent must *never* be ashamed to request a reduction or scholarship for the Torah education of their children. To emphasize once again, the entire enterprise of a Torah education for children was, and still is, a collective one.

The goal of having many children and managing to fully educate them has successfully been achieved in the modern era countless times.

Had we been witness to hundreds of children from large Jewish families roaming the streets (or attending public schools) due to lack of funds for Jewish schooling, there would admittedly need to be a rather different discussion. To date, this is not the case in any country in the world. It is true that in countries where parents must bear the bulk of the cost, many or most Jewish children do not attend a Jewish school. Ironically though, the clear majority of these cases are those where family size is not very large at all. In contrast, those communities that emphasize the value of large families also manage to fully educate

---

18    Ibid., 3.
19    Ibid.

practically all of their children in schools, yeshivos, and seminaries. Put simply, if there's a will there's a way.

In the final analysis, the success of raising large families in modern times has come when families with a more limited income have followed the module prescribed above, which includes:

- Budgeting family expenditures
- Putting in the maximum effort toward earnings
- Sending the children to schools that
  - are subsidized by both individuals and the community,
  - share both the values of having large families and of educating every Jewish child in their midst.

The justification, merits, and tremendous benefits of leading such a lifestyle has been the running theme of this work.

As emphasized earlier, a principle in Judaism says that it is G-d's will for the needs of a person to reach them through a natural process. It can be hardly called a "natural process" if a person expects sufficient funds to suddenly and magically appear in their bank account on the day a child walks through the doors of a day school, yeshiva, or seminary. This does not mean that parents will always be able to save for the full tuition expenses of all their children. But, as said above, the Torah obligates a person to do their part in fulfilling their own responsibilities, and not to rely on the community—or a miracle—to foot the bill.

Young parents must understand that effort in income and budgeting expenditures may need to begin long before a tuition bill arrives. After all, can a couple take the liberty of deciding at which point G-d will begin to grant them the means to educate their children?

Another important application of this involves priority. The Code of Jewish Law is clear that when it comes to charity, the first and primary obligation of a Jew is to the members of his own family.[20] Coupled with the Torah's mandate to continue having children, the outcome is

---

20    *Shulchan Aruch, Yoreh Deah, Hilchos Tzedakah* 251:3.

simple: the education of one's children, additional ones included, must be properly met before resource and time can be devoted to other worthy, charitable causes.

One concrete application of the above is that in many instances a person may use money of *maaser* (the tenth of one's earnings usually given to charity) to pay for their child's Torah education. The halachic opinions about this matter vary, and a rabbi should be consulted for guidance, but the concept in itself is halachically firm and accepted.

In closing, a well-known Talmudic passage tells us that although overspending is not advisable, as we can never know if G-d will add to our allocated income, adding to the expenditure for the Torah learning of a child is different. [21] At some point and in some way, the Almighty will ensure that a parent will always be able to meet their financial commitments in this area:

> *A person's entire livelihood is allocated to them during the period from Rosh Hashanah to Yom Kippur, with the exception of expenditures for Shabbos, expenditures for the Festivals, and expenditures for his sons' Torah study. In these areas, no exact amount is determined; rather, if he reduced the amount he spends for these purposes, his income is reduced, and if he increased his expenditures in these areas, his income is increased."* [22]

## WHEN THE GOING GETS TOUGH

Sometimes, a situation can arise in which there is no foreseeable way for a family to bear their financial burden alone. This may have nothing to do with lack of will or effort on the part of the parents. Sometimes a situation (such as illness, G-d forbid) can befall a family, rendering the financial burden simply impossible to bear without help.

---

21  Classically, a person is only obligated to teach their son Torah. See, however, *Igros Moshe, Yoreh Deah* 2:113, who considers the education of a daughter in our time to also be a complete obligation. It is at least plausible to assert that today, the Talmudic concept herein extends to the education of both male and female children.

22  *Beitzah* 16a. See *Rashi* there.

The final section of this book will touch upon the fact that, sometimes, severe financial stress is a cause to seek the counsel of a rabbi regarding the feasibility of having additional children. Such a situation however, may occur to a family that is already large in number. There are some important points to be made in this regard.

As elaborated upon earlier, the emphatic position of Torah is that every child is infinitely necessary and precious in the eyes of G-d. The birth of every child is meticulously planned by G-d Himself Who so willed it that this child be born to precisely these parents and at precisely this time. It is crucial for parents or onlookers to internalize that children are the ultimate form of riches and privilege. The fact that they may need to temporarily rely on help from others is because it has been so decided on High for reasons that are far beyond the comprehension of any mortal.

The Talmud recounts: "Turnus Rufus the wicked[23] asked Rabbi Akiva, 'If your G-d loves the poor, for what reason does He not support them?' Rabbi Akiva said to him, 'He commands us to sustain the poor, so that through them, we will be saved from the judgment in the World to Come.'"[24] This response of Rabbi Akiva does not justify the suffering of the poor, but rather shapes the attitude both for the giver of charity and for the one compelled to receive it. In the words of the midrash: "More than the benefactor does unto the poor man, the poor man does unto the benefactor."[25]

All the above would be true even if we were not to take into consideration the actions of these children or young people in need. In most cases, these children will be good people and devoted Jews, whose daily mitzvos are invaluable and indispensable to the Jewish people and the world at large. "Be careful with the sons of the poor," warns the Talmud, "as it is from them that the Torah will issue forth."[26] The well-being of every child is far from just being the project of his or her parents; it is the project of the Jewish people at large.

---

23    A general in the Roman army who caused much suffering to the Jewish people.
24    *Bava Basra* 10a.
25    *Midrash Rabbah Rus* 5:9.
26    *Nedarim* 81a.

Having said this, it must be emphasized that, when possible, a family compelled to accept charity should never resign itself to this fate. In cases where this applies, continuous efforts should be made to reduce or eliminate the need to rely on such support. "Make your Shabbos like an ordinary weekday," instructs the Talmud, "and do not be beholden onto others."[27]

## A HELPING FAMILY

While on the subject of external help, it should be noted that there is one area not included in the discussion of financial burdens above. We refer here to both financial as well as other forms of assistance from parents (or immediate family). It is a most healthy and praiseworthy dynamic for parents to assist their children in the venture of building a family of their own. Having children, or additional children, is a fundamentally important and sacred task in a person's early life, equal at least to the other areas in which parents assist their children in becoming fully established.

As part of this, it is also important to note the role that grandparents play in the support of their grandchildren. The Code of Jewish Law states that the Torah education of a grandchild is at the very least a charitable priority for a grandparent. In certain circumstances, it can even take the form of an actual obligation.[28] By extension, grandparents should see it as a joy and privilege to assist their grandchildren in establishing a vibrant Jewish home. The perspective of the grandchildren should be the same.

## THE PATH OF THE RIGHTEOUS

The Talmud records an argument between Rabbi Yishmael and Rabbi Shimon bar Yochai: Rabbi Yishmael contends that while one is obligated to make time to study Torah, a person must nevertheless go about the "way of the world" in the pursuit of making a living. Rabbi Shimon, on

---

27    *Pesachim* 112a.

28    See *Shulchan Aruch HaRav* ibid., 8–9.

the other hand, insists that a Jew must devote himself entirely to Torah and, in doing so, "his work will be performed by others."

Analyzing this argument, the Talmudic Sage Abaye commented: "Many acted in accordance with Rabbi Yishmael and were successful, and many have acted in accordance with Rabbi Shimon bar Yochai and were not successful."[29]

On a practical level, the Jewish position has always been that there is indeed room for both ways of life. Throughout our history, there have been many Jews who sacrificed even a basic standard of living for the sake of Torah learning or community work. The "work performed by others," or the little work they did themselves, would be just enough for them to get by. For the average person, such an action is classified as *middas chassidus*—an act of piety. It is something the Torah puts out as a possibility, but not as an obligation. It is important to understand that the Torah does give this choice to a Jew, and if he so chooses to live this way, the Torah fully sanctions such a way of life.[30]

As the Talmud states, however, it is often the case that people fail in standing up to the ramifications of their own initial decisions. Great care must be taken not to misread the level of one's own spiritual devotion. In this sense, the Code of Jewish Law warns that making a choice of piety without being sufficiently prepared to do so can backlash, eventually leading the person to "act against the will of his Maker."[31]

If finance is being voiced as a concern for the decision to have more children by a couple who has chosen a certain level of pious lifestyle, then this itself may be indicative that some self-reevaluation may be in order.

As has been emphasized and will be elaborated upon below, the value and necessity of an additional child overrides many otherwise noble spiritual causes. An affirmative decision of both having another child and maintaining a certain pious lifestyle must be made with the full knowledge and commitment to all ramifications of this resolution.

---

29    *Berachos* 35b.

30    See *Shulchan Aruch HaRav, Hilchos Talmud Torah* 3:4.

31    *Shulchan Aruch, Orach Chaim* 156:1.

An additional level of caution seems to be in place in our day and age: the joy and readiness of the children themselves to join their parents in living a life of piety has a direct effect on their future spiritual well-being. Parents must gauge this carefully and make their decisions accordingly.

CHAPTER 9

# *Inconvenience*

## A LIFE OF FULFILLMENT

The simple truth is that when considering both time and money, having additional children usually limits the personal aspirations of parents. In an age when so much of the culture is centered around the "self," the intensity of this issue is obviously magnified.

To begin, we would do well with reiterating what we have endeavored to demonstrate in the first part of this book. Another child is the embodiment of the entire purpose of creation and the purpose of one's own descent to this world. The opportunity and ability of having another child is the surest indication that this child is a major and integral part in fulfilling one's own purpose in life. Moreover, there is nothing more precious and valuable a Jew can ever wish for than the gift of another Jewish child.

The first, and possibly foremost, element of addressing this concern is the encouragement to internalize that having a child is the highest form of *self-fulfillment*. Nothing can magnify a parent's own purpose and being more than this.

With G-d's help, a child will live on after their parents and continue their legacy. They will impact this world in many untold ways. Simply put, the effort and sacrifice of raising a child has *infinite* and *eternal* return. To grossly understate things, every child is entirely "worth it."

Only after establishing the ideas above can we begin addressing the concern at hand.

One of the great principles of Judaism is that "[Of] everything the Holy One Blessed Be He created in His world, He did not create anything in vain."[1] Everything in this world has a purpose. Insofar as the person is concerned, having a certain talent or aspiration is itself an indication that they should channel it for doing good.

What is important to understand is that the use of talent and fulfillment of aspiration is but one aspect of our purpose in this world. Life, especially for the Jew, is multi-faceted and full of contradictory responsibilities. Each part of this variation is integral to the construction of our physical and spiritual well-being.

It is often tempting to overstep the boundaries and ignore one important aspect of life on the account of another. Truthfully, however, we know that this is never beneficial. As an example, our Sages warn us that "one who says he has nothing other than Torah, he does not have Torah either."[2] Studying is important, but doing good is also important. They are both mandated to us from the one and only G-d.

It is clear that both having another child and fulfilling one's aspirations and talents are both important. Time should be made for both. The injunction of having another child coupled with the instruction of using one's talents is itself the indication that both can be done. If G-d had something else in store for them, a couple would not be presented with the opportunity of having another child (or altogether been given this mitzvah). To be sure, regardless of what a couple may plan at the onset, the question of whether another child will actually be conceived is altogether up to G-d.

Finally, it is crucial to remember that, ultimately, success and fulfillment

---

1    *Shabbos* 77b.
2    *Yevamos* 109b.

is not about the quantity of time spent on an endeavor, but about the quality and impact we have. By doing what the Almighty asks of us, we can feel assured that the smaller amount of time and energy invested in personal aspirations will possess the security and blessing that "G-d's presence will reside in your work."[3] Assuredly, there can be no greater wish for any area of human endeavor or enterprise.

The discussion above leads into another important area, the question of if, or to what degree, a mother of young children should work (for pay) outside the home.

The reality in many households is that there is a genuine need for an additional income other than that of the father. Aside from this, it is often important for the mother to work for the purpose of her own well-being. Great care must be taken, however, that the professional life of a mother should not infringe on her primary mission, namely, being the *akeres ha'bayis*, the mainstay and bedrock of the home.

This caution is not exclusive to a mother. A father must similarly be cautious to remain highly focused on the well-being and upbringing of his children. But remaining true to her primary role, a mother will always need to devote more time and attention to her children, especially when they are younger. It must be powerfully clear in the mind of a mother that care for her children is the most sacred task and deepest privilege she could possibly wish for. Fulfilling this task properly must take priority. The daily decisions of work and family must have this value at their core.

## WHAT CREATES SPIRITUAL GREATNESS

As mentioned in the introduction, concern about the inconvenience additional children entail can also be of a spiritual nature—concern about the lack of time and focus in Torah study, prayer, or community service.

---

3    See *Rashi* for *Shemos* 39:43.

Torah study and mitzvah performance are most certainly sacred, but a person must be careful not to fall into the trap of playing G-d. We are taught that the *yetzer hara* (the evil impulse), can disguise itself in many forms, and great wisdom is needed to perceive its machinations. It may clothe itself in the garb of an earnest, straightforward, humble *tzaddik*, arousing devotion toward a holy cause. The truth is, however, that this is nothing more than the *yetzer hara's* theatrics, trying to prevent the person from engaging in their intended mission.

As explained in the first part of this work, the deepest and most essential desire of G-d is a physical Jew here on earth. Our Sages state in the midrash, "There are two things in the world... Torah and the Jewish people. Yet I do not know which is first: I told him the way of people is to say that the Torah came first, yet I say the Jewish people came first."[4]

It goes without saying that the bond between G-d and the Jewish people can only be revealed and be made apparent through Torah study and spiritual pursuits. At the heart of the matter, though, is that the Torah is there for the Jew and not the Jew for the Torah.[5] One of the applications of this is when the interest of "Torah"—either Torah study or other spiritual endeavors—seem, at least on the surface, to clash with the interest of bringing another Jew into this world. To G-d, the life of another Jew is supreme. Being in the position of ability to have another child indicates that G-d has entrusted the couple in question with this most lofty of missions. To be sure, as explained above at length, not only is another child not a contradiction to one's own spiritual elevation, it is the be-all and end-all of all spiritual and G-dly pursuits. It may not immediately feel this way, but this is the fact.

Having said this, it is crucial for a parent to rest assured that if it is their destiny to fulfill a certain spiritual tak or accomplish a certain goal, they will never lose out by having additional children.

Success in any project, whether physical or spiritual in nature, necessitates Divine blessing. Following the will of G-d in having additional

---

4    *Tanna D'bei Eliyahu Rabbah*, chap. 14.
5    See at length *Likutei Sichos*, vol. 34, p. 217 ff.

children will ensure that the time and energy invested in any project will indeed be blessed in this way.

An important addition to the above is that the choice of having another child brings gain to the parents in the area of Torah study and mitzvah performance *itself*.

The Talmud tells us that although a woman does not have the same level of obligation in Torah study as a man, nevertheless, "in reward for causing their sons to read Torah and learn the Mishnah, and for waiting for their husbands until they come home from the study hall, do they not share the reward with their sons and husbands?"[6]

In other words, facilitating the Torah study of a child allows the parent a share in this very mitzvah. This concept may well be extended to other mitzvos done by children but facilitated by parents.

This is an idea truly worthy of contemplation. True, the amounts of time and energy needed to care for children are great. But in the facilitation of a child's Torah learning and mitzvah performance, a parent is spiritually growing and ascending *through the child*. As explained above, the Torah study and mitzvos of children holds incredible specialty even over the Torah and mitzvos of adults. This adds an extra dimension to the above idea.

Often, a parent may feel spiritual frustration in having to be submerged and consumed in the endless tasks necessary in sustaining a large family.

This too touches on a most basic and fundamental Torah concept. It is crucial that parents of a large family never feel bad or wronged by the fact that much of their time and strength must be devoted to working and dealing with the physical and menial.

As elaborated upon above, the very purpose of Creation itself is that

---

6    *Sotah* 21a. See *Shulchan Aruch Harav, Hilchos Talmud Torah* 1:14.

the soul should descend to this world and make *this world* a place for G-d. This is done by working in the world and utilizing it for holiness. For some, this goal is achieved by saturating their physical mind and heart with G-dliness. However, the ultimate fashion in which the purpose of creation is fulfilled is through working with and elevating the physical and material world *itself*.

Moreover, just as one should view an additional child as a gift from G-d, so too should providing for this child be seen as a privilege and a sacred task. To be sure, the birth of another child contains within it the indication that providing for it characterizes a primary part of the parents' mission here on earth.

The Torah fully recognizes that physical life may account for the great majority of a Jew's time and energy. This is why when it comes to Torah study, although there is an obligation on every Jew to study, there is no obligatory amount of time he must set aside for this. This rather depends on how much time the person is able to set aside. One major factor in this is his family size.[7]

The challenge the Torah *does* give to the working Jew is contained in the verse of *Tehillim* quoted above: "When you eat the labor of your hands, you are praiseworthy."[8] Our Sages tell us that the terminology here is carefully chosen; work should involve a Jew's "hands" but not his "head." In most cases, it is obvious that a person must also immerse their minds in their work. The idea here is that a person should only immerse his more external level of mind in work and not allow it to penetrate their inner and fundamental consciousness. In the times set for learning, prayer, and mitzvah performance, a person should be able to entirely free themselves from involvement in work and be completely immersed in holiness.

---

7    See *Shulchan Aruch HaRav, Hilchos Talmud Torah* 3:1.

8    *Tehillim* 128:2.

CHAPTER 10

# Strain and Anxiety

## PHYSICAL AND EMOTIONAL STRAIN

Properly raising children demands huge amounts of physical, mental, and emotional strength. Actually, the very concept of hard work is associated in Judaism with the labor of raising children.

The text of the Passover haggadah expounds on a verse that sums up the story of slavery and Exodus from Egypt. "G-d saw...our travails," it states.[1] This, says the haggadah, is a reference to "the children." Unlike many of its other expositions, the haggadah brings no scriptural evidence for the fact that "our travail" is actually a reference to children. It takes it for granted that the association of children and hard work is self-evident, even synonymous.

Good things demand hard work. As a rule, the greater the cause, the more work it takes to achieve it. As we have sought to establish, children constitute the highest possible cause for a parent.

What remains to be clarified from a conceptual standpoint is why this is so: Why must having children be so physically and emotionally taxing?

---

1    *Devarim* 26:7.

In view of its centrality, why did the Creator choose to make this project so difficult? The understanding of this is central for the motivation and morale of parents, especially those considering having another child.

The question is quite broad as it encompasses many important but difficult facets of life. The verse has been quoted before as stating that "man is born to toil."[2] But why must this be the case? If G-d is good, why did He make such important elements of our mission on earth so difficult?

Our Sages point out that human nature dictates that a person will only take pleasure in that which they created through their own work: "A person desires one measure of his own more than nine measures of his fellow."[3] Indeed, the more toil a person invests, the sweeter the fruits of that labor are to him. In contrast, a person will naturally feel degraded if they are handed a reward without doing anything adequate to earn it. Our Sages call it "bread of shame."[4] G-d is good and desires that man take genuine contentment from fulfilling his mission here on earth. Therefore, He necessitated that man fulfill his purpose through his own toil and labor.

The question, however, can still be asked: granted that man only derives real satisfaction from his own work, but is G-d not the Creator of man as well? Why is it that man is only destined to be satisfied in such a way?

The Hebrew name of the first man was Adam, which can also be translated as "mankind." The root of the word Adam is the same as the Hebrew term *domeh*—similar to or the likeness of. The fabric of a human being is to be similar to or in the likeness of his Creator.

Man could have been given everything necessary without the need for effort. But G-d gave us something greater. He made us in a way that we should not only be creations, i.e., recipients, but allowed us to possess an element of the Creator, i.e., the ability to contribute. In the words of our Sages, we have the ability of being "a partner to G-d in the works of creation."[5] Had we been simply given all that we needed in

---

2    *Iyov* 5:7.
3    *Bava Metziah* 38a.
4    See *Talmud Yerushalmi Orlah* 1:3.
5    *Shabbos* 119b.

fulfilling our mission on earth, we would remain recipients of G-d, not partners to Him. G-d created the world in a way that is unfinished so that we could become His partners.

The midrash tells us:

> *A philosopher asked Rabbi Hoshaya: If G-d so loves circumcision, why did he not give it to Adam [i.e., why was man not born circumcised]?*
>
> *He said to him: Anything created in the first six days, needs further action. For example, mustard seeds need sweetening, peas need sweetening, wheat needs grinding; even humans need fixing.*[6]

Nothing physically or spiritually valuable is just handed to us. The world was created in such a way that in every aspect of life, we enter a partnership with the Almighty in bringing the world from the place it is to the place it is meant to be.

In the realm of human endeavor, there is no greater exercise in partnering with G-d than the creation of a new child and the maintenance of its well-being. It is here that the parents partner with G-d, not only in a detail of the creation, but in that which encapsulates the entirety of creation itself. This may well be the reason why the project of having a child is *synonymous* with hard work: one and together, they both epitomize the great partnership between G-d and mankind.

The hard work that accompanies raising children can be taxing. It is never easy. Yet it is the difficulty of the project itself that is the demonstration of its primal significance.

Having said all this, it is of great importance to recognize that the workload of properly raising additional children does not have to belong exclusively to the parents.

As with all other areas in life, there are basic elements of our existence

---

6    *Midrash Rabbah Bereishis* 11.

that are often outsourced to a third party. The more responsibilities a person assumes outside of their own immediate survival, the more they can—and must—allow for other parties to provide them with their basic necessities.

The great amount of time and effort needed in raising additional children is the best of justifications for the outsourcing of domestic chores. A person should not feel inadequate by needing to hire additional help in the home, or seeking various other forms of domestic assistance. As elaborated upon earlier, maintaining a stable and respectable lifestyle is crucial to the fulfillment of one's entire mission here on earth, and is certainly necessary to successfully raise mentally, emotionally, and spiritually healthy children. The necessary funds needed for this can certainly be seen as part of the bounty granted by G-d with the addition of every child.

As should be self-understood, the above does not absolve parents of their responsibility to personally give the necessary attention and devotion to their children. On the contrary: the outsourcing of domestic and similar chores allows both parents, and particularly the mother, to devote themselves more fully and efficiently to the upbringing of the children. Being a parent is something that no third party can ever replace.

A closing thought on this matter can be drawn from the words of the Mishnah:

> One who accepts upon himself the yoke of Torah, the yoke of
> government and the yoke of 'the way of the world' is lifted from
> him. But one who casts from himself the yoke of Torah, the
> yoke of government and the yoke of 'the way of the world' is
> placed upon him.[7]

It seems that one way or the other, man is destined to bear some sort of yoke. The choice has been given, however, as to which yoke this will

---

7    *Avos* 3:5.

be. Choosing the "yoke of Torah"—the effort associated with following the Torah way—frees a person from many other "yokes," genuine or imaginary, that may have otherwise been their lot.

Altogether, it remains up to the person to realize that this "yoke" is in fact the vehicle for their true liberation, fulfillment, and joy, both in this world and in the next.

## FEAR AND ANXIETY

Having a child sets in motion a process that runs entirely into the unknown. The uncertainty can be daunting. What is it that can give potential parents the emotional strength to take the plunge and have another?

Below are some points for contemplation:

- Life is uncertain. Yet very little can match the ability of turning Heavenward and saying, "We have done that which you have instructed us; now You do what is incumbent upon You to do."[8] The relationship between G-d and the Jewish people is characterized in the words of King Solomon as, "I am to my Beloved, and my Beloved is to me."[9] Devoting ourselves to doing what G-d wants of us means that G-d is there for us. G-d watches over all His creations, but those who are devoted to doing His will and make sacrifices for doing so are understandably in an entirely different league. "The feet of His pious ones He will guard," says the verse.[10] The joy and security that is generated by this realization is unparalleled; it is the knowledge that regardless of life's circumstances we have nothing to fear. "Though I walk through the valley of the shadow of death, I will fear no evil, for You are with me."[11]

- A foundational idea of Torah is the simple instruction of "don't

---

8    See *Rashi Devarim* 26:15.
9    *Shir Hashirim* 6:3.
10   *Shmuel I* 2:9.
11   *Tehillim* 23:4.

worry." "Cast your burden on G-d and He will sustain you."[12] Worrying never helps, but trusting in G-d does. This pertains to any area of life, but all the more so when the matter at hand is the nearest and dearest thing to G-d Himself. Raising a child is certainly not something we do on our own. More than anything else, this is totally and entirely G-d's "business."

- Our Sages tell us: "The Holy One Blessed Be He does not deal imperiously [i.e., unreasonably] with His creatures." Or, as it is put elsewhere: "I [G-d] do not ask according to My strength but according to theirs."[13] G-d does not ask us to do the impossible. Taking each step and day one at a time, we can rest assured that we possess the full ability of succeeding.

---

12   *Tehillim* 55:23.
13   *Avodah Zarah* 3a; *Bamidbar Rabbah* 12:3.

CHAPTER 11

# Other Concerns

## PARENTAL COMPETENCE

"But I'm not the ideal parent!" Some do not see raising children as their expertise or specialty. Yet having another child is not a mitzvah just for those who are in love with kids.

Before we begin, it should also be noted that—as with every project and endeavor—the more practice a person has, the better they become at it. Raising children is no different: the skills and experience gained with previous children will undoubtedly make having another both easier and more efficient in multiple ways.

As can be readily deduced from our discussion so far, having another child is not merely a detail, an avenue for the fulfillment of one's Divine mission. Rather, it is a *mitzvah klalis*—a general and foundational mitzvah, touching the very essence and purpose of our being in this world.

G-d made man to be perfect at nothing, including the tasks of parenthood. By virtue of being human, every parent will be at least somewhat flawed. Mistakes will be made. Rectifying one's character and working with one's own shortcomings is a life-long project that will reach far beyond the time that we are called upon to raise children.

Yet this is what life is all about. G-d created us precisely in the way we are, for He wants us to do our best according to our current level of character and ability. To quote the above-mentioned Talmudic phrase: "I [G-d] do not ask according to My strength but according to theirs."

The Talmud tells us that Rabbi Yehudah Hanasi, the great Sage and author of the Mishnah, would "honor the wealthy."[1] One of the reasons given for this is that being wealthy is a demonstration that G-d trusts this particular person with using their riches properly. The wealthy individual possesses special qualities, or else he would not be entrusted with this unique task. Similarly, having another child is the greatest demonstration of G-d's confidence in a couple and the fact that they have the capabilities of living up to this expectation.

Our Sages tell us that "one who comes to purify is assisted [from Above]."[2] The obvious starting point for the challenged parent is to study the teachings of the Torah connected to this subject. On a practical level, properly raising children is similar to most valuable things in life—it takes attention and effort and should be accompanied with an ongoing quest to improve. Nothing stands in the way of genuine will. Once we have the will, we can all find a way.

Finally, the Torah guarantees that "according to the effort is the reward."[3] The more difficult a mitzvah is, the more valuable it becomes.

## THE CHILDREN THEMSELVES

In considering the birth of another child, concern may be raised for the other children who will now be part of a larger family. After all, children in larger families will usually have less unique parental attention and will tend to enjoy fewer comforts and leisure.

The first question we must address is whether children of larger families are automatically losing out on any *necessary* or *important* component of either their upbringing or their adult life. If parents are investing on a level that a parent should, are children from large

---

1   *Eruvin* 86a.
2   *Yoma* 38b.
3   *Avos* 5:21.

families at a disadvantage? The answer coming from several major and recent studies is: not necessarily.

Studies in previous decades demonstrated how children in larger families achieve lower grades in school than their peers in smaller families. In the late 1990s, however, American sociologist Douglas Downey found that the presence of certain parental resources in the family practically eliminated this lack of performance:

> *The parental resources producing the largest reduction of the effect of sibship size[4] on educational performance are (in order): frequency of talk, parents' educational expectations, money saved for college, and educational objects in the home. Indeed, including just these four indicators for parental resources is enough to reduce the effect of sibship size on grades to non-significance."[5]*

The idea that children in large families are not automatically disadvantaged was supported by another piece of research in which the outcomes for children in large families differed largely from one country to another:

> *[I]n India and China, as in the US, having more siblings lowers children's educational attainment, whereas in Israel and Norway, there is no negative association between family size and schooling when careful statistical techniques are used.*

The explanation for this finding, given by the researchers themselves, lies in several factors such as access to public (or communal) safety nets, good education, and importantly, the norms and social integration of a family's community.[6] To quote Douglas Downy again: "In highly integrated communities with norms supporting large families...studies

---

4   The scholarly term for the number of siblings in a family.

5   D. Downey, "Why Bigger Is Not Better," *American Sociological Review*, vol. 60 (1995): 746–61.

6   Anna Sutherland, "For Kids, Large Families Have Pros and Cons," Institute for Family Studies, January 6, 2016. https://ifstudies.org/blog/for-kids-large-families-have-pros-and-cons.

find only weak relationships between sibship size and educational outcomes."[7]

The encouragement of Torah to have many children is within the context of how the Torah constructs Jewish life in general. The values of family, community, and education are front and center to everything the Jewish people hold holy and dear. Putting these values to work, a Jewish couple can be confident that their additional children will have the same opportunities as any other child.

Although the evidence is clear that children will not necessarily be disadvantaged for being part of a larger family, it may nevertheless be difficult for a parent to accept their inability to give more to an individual child. Below are some ideas for consideration.

The desire to give more attention and time to a child is incredibly virtuous. With a larger family, this need not be compromised, but rather, compacted. "Quality time" is the key. The preference of quality over quantity should be extended not to the number of children but to the level of involvement with them. It is not what we give our children, but the way in which we give it.

This is the concept of "success in time." Many matters of importance are achievable in less time. Working smart is just as important as working hard, and maybe even more so.

Now, this is not to say that a parent can compromise on the quantity of parental attention necessary in the life of a child. A parent

---

7    Anna Sutherland, "Are Smaller Families Better for Kids? It Depends," Institute for Family Studies, November 21, 2013. https://ifstudies.org/blog/are-smaller-families-better-for-kids-it-depends.

In general, the "Resource Dilution Model," the theory that more children will result in poorer outcomes, has been recently challenged by a growing number of academics. In 2010, the authors of a Dutch demographic study wrote: "Resource dilution theory predicts that with larger sibship size, children's status outcome falls. However, the empirical record has shown that this is not always the case…The negative effect of sibship size has been found to be much weaker, neutral, or even positive." Hilde Bras, Jan Kok, and Kees Mandemakers, "Sibship Size and Status Attainment," *Demographic Research*, vol. 23 (July 2010), 73–104.

must carefully gauge this need and answer it adequately. But the time spent together—either with an individual child or with the family as a whole—can be charged with more devotion and love, which makes this time meaningful in the first place. In our case, it can also fill the desire for more quantity of time as well.[8]

The above is also applicable when speaking of a parent's desire to give more attention to the spiritual development of their children: the mitzvah of continuing to have children makes it evident that the will of the Almighty is the quality of educational investment, rather than the quantity.

Children are, in a very large way, an outgrowth of their environment. Having the children in a loving and happy atmosphere of devotion to G-d, Torah, and the Jewish people, is the surest way of empowering them to seek the expansion of their own spiritual horizons.

As to the concern for children of larger families having less opportunities for comfort, extracurricular activities, leisure, and the like, the following can be said:

To the thinking parent, the lack of some of these extras are aspects of *blessing* in a culture of increasing entitlement and narcissism among young people. From a young age, children in a larger family are acutely aware that the world does not revolve around them. They learn to enjoy the simple but beautiful things in life. As they grow older, they will usually take things less for granted, a trait which will unarguably stand them in good stead in multiple ways.

## THE ENVIRONMENT

As mentioned in our introduction, limiting family size has been overwhelmingly sanctioned in public opinion due to the question of

---

8    It is worthy of noting that several recent studies strongly question the notion that increased amounts of parental involvement effects significant change in a child. Bryan Caplan, in his book *Selfish Reasons to Have More Kids* (Basic Books, 2011), compiles much of the research as it connects to the question of having additional children.

overpopulation and human sustainability. Can Judaism continue to encourage the birth of many children despite these serious concerns?

It is well-known that in its capacity as a manual for life, the Torah has a dual system: one for the Jew, and the other for the rest of humanity. As will be elaborated on at the end of this work, one of the aspects where this finds expression is in the area of procreation. The conclusion of the early Talmudic and halachic authorities is that while the encouragement to have children is universal, the *commandment* for having children remains an imperative only to the Jew.[9]

Whether or not the Torah did this in order to forestall a population issue is a subject for speculation. The net result, however, of the Torah system has a conclusive bearing on this discussion.

The Torah itself attests to the fact that Jews are "the smallest among all the nations."[10] This has remained true throughout the centuries. To date, the Jewish people constitute less than one fifth of one percent of the world population. An increase in the size of Jewish families, while vital for Jewish survival, cannot be considered as part of a conversation on population and environmental issues.

The Jewish people is characterized in the Torah as a "kingdom of priests and a holy nation."[11] Throughout the Torah we read at great length about the special regulations and lifestyle that was to be kept by the Kohanim, the selected priestly family within the Jewish people themselves. The Divine intention, however, was that the Kohanim should be unique in this. Both their privileges and responsibilities are not to be duplicated by the rest of the people.[12]

Each person is created by G-d with a unique and specific purpose. Biblically, the purpose of the Kohanim (or on a broader scale, the tribe of Levi) was to be the spiritual backbone of the people. They taught the people Torah and brought them close to G-d in the Temple service. As for the rest of the people, they were not meant to be Kohanim. It was

---

9   See *Aruch Hashulchan, Even Haezer* 1:5.

10   *Devarim* 7:7.

11   *Shemos* 19:6.

12   The Biblical story of Korach and its devastating results were the demonstration of this important concept.

their mission to take the learning and inspiration they received from the Kohanim and bring it into the world by living and working in a holy way.

In a broader sense, the Jewish people are to be the "priests" on the global scale. The Jew is charged with being the spiritual nexus of the world and to set the example in this regard. As a result, the Jew has responsibilities and lifestyle that are not the same for the rest of humanity, who have a very different function. Many (though not all) of the ideas discussed in this book about the centrality of having another child are unique to the Jewish people.

An issue of importance that has recently entered the Jewish conversation is the population concern in the Land of Israel. As opposed to the old question of a large Arab base or even majority in the land, this conversation has been centered around the concern relating to rapid growth in Israel as a whole and whether this is sustainable going forward in view of the country's limited space and resources.

From a Torah perspective there are two major ideas to keep in mind:

- The Jewish people are not a nation that answers to natural law. Our existence and survival are altogether unnatural, and being where we are today in the Land of Israel against all the odds is a historic and ongoing miracle of miracles. It is a fact of history that regardless of attempts made, no other people were ever able to settle and build the Land of Israel aside for us, the Jewish people. Our Sages tell us that not only are the people of Israel not governed by nature, but even the very Land of Israel itself is above the laws of nature. With regard to Eretz Yisrael, it is written: "Land of the deer" (*Yirmiyahu* 3:19). "Just as the skin of a deer cannot hold its flesh, for after the animal is skinned, its hide shrinks, so too, with regard to Eretz Yisrael, when it is settled, it expands, but when it is not settled, it contracts."[13] Somehow, the Land of Israel will never be too small for its people.

---

13   *Gittin* 57a. See *Gevuros Hashem* 24:5.

- Bearing this in mind, we are nevertheless instructed not to rely on miracles. As a people, we must do our part in making sure our land is safe and prosperous. The point of departure, however, must be clear: no plan for sustainability in the Land of Israel must ever have the shrinking of the Jewish people at its center. Not only would this be a spiritual and historic slap in the face, but the repercussions for such a policy could be serious indeed—in view of the hostility to Israel both from within and from without, the staggering level of assimilation of Jews in the diaspora, the economic factor—just to name a few. Thankfully, the school of thought in many academic circles has centered around original ideas of putting technology and planning to work in a way that can sustain population growth.[14]

To conceptualize about a future where all the ideas have been maximized and we have no other choice has historically been proven foolish. As one Jewish writer recently put it:

> *The nay-sayers who forecasted that the world would run out of food many years ago were wrong, the same as those forecasting that population growth is unsustainable. We have found new ways to grow food, to quadruple harvests, to have productive greenhouses in barren areas and even to plant vertical gardens against hi-rise buildings.*
>
> *Was it conceivable years ago that Israel would have desalination plants in a country that used to be barren? What is missing in the calculations of the great experts who predict doom and gloom is faith: faith in ourselves to find solutions, and faith in G-d.*[15]

---

14    See Avi Temkin, "למדינה צפופה במזרח התיכון דרושים אמצעי מניעה", *Globes.co.il*, December 17, 2018, https://www.globes.co.il/news/article.aspx?did=1001231961.
15    Leonie Ben-Simon," Overpopulation—Really?" *The Jerusalem Post*, Feburary 28, 2018. https://www.jpost.com/Opinion/Overpopulation-really-543928.

## COSMETIC CONCERNS

The effect on the appearance of a mother due to her pregnancy and birth may be a discouraging factor when considering having another child. To be sure, there may be less to worry about than anticipated. In recent years there has been a wonderful expansion in choice of maternity and postpartum clothing, making the transition easier and even pleasurable. In addition, many even experience a kind of "pregnancy glow" during these months. This said, there may be still those to whom their appearance during and after pregnancy is of concern to them. Although this may be approached from several possible angles (some of which we have covered above), there is an additional, rather interesting approach to this particular subject.

Being accustomed to a certain level of pleasure actually causes the resulting good feelings to become unexciting. "Constant pleasure is not pleasure."[16] This is true of any pleasure of life, and beauty is no different. It is actually accentuated in the area of beauty, since beauty has very much to do with the "eyes of the beholder."

Pregnancy and post-pregnancy do not last forever. In this way, there is a renewed joy for the woman herself, her husband, and all others concerned with the return of the mother's regular appearance, apparel, etc. After an initial absence, this return will make all hearts grow fonder.

This idea is reflected in another area of Torah that is highly related to our subject: The laws of *niddah,* the time during and after menstruation when husband and wife refrain from physical contact, are part of the laws of *tumah* and *taharah* (ritual purity or impurity) for which the Torah does not give a readily understandable explanation. Nevertheless, our Sages posit that there is an incredible benefit in these laws, as they uphold a crucial element of marriage—namely, the renewed excitement of husband and wife with one another.

> *[It is] so in order that she should be more beloved to her husband in the proper, felicitous time, and they should not grow disgusted with one another on account of too great constancy*

---

16    See *Keser Shem Tov* 1:121.

*of their closeness, thus casting their eyes on other bodies, as do most of the nations who are not bound by our stringent "fences" (protective restrictions).[17]*

King Solomon writes: "I saw that wisdom has an advantage over folly, as the advantage of light over darkness."[18] One of the meanings in this is that the value of light is only appreciated when there is a knowledge—or actual experience—of darkness. The same is true with wisdom and folly; when foolishness abounds, we appreciate the value of wisdom. This is many times the *purpose* of a dark situation—to allow the light to be even more valued and cherished.

After a period of it being less so, the restored beauty of a woman is all the more valued and appreciated. Countless Jewish couples attest to the Divine genius that lies in the *niddah* laws by creating the initial void that keeps their love and attraction so alive. The concept, as it pertains to pregnancy and childbirth, is the same.

Admittedly, there are those women who may complain that after multiple pregnancies, they were not able to return to their ideal, pre-pregnancy look. In this regard it must be remembered that just as there are Jewish riches, there is also Jewish beauty. Much to the admiration of so many, the spiritual dignity and distinction of a true Jewish woman carries over to her physical appearance in the most literal way.

To quote King Solomon again, "The wisdom of a person illuminates his face."[19] The inner joy and deep fulfilment in raising her precious children is the source for both the visible and inner grace of a Jewish woman.

## SOCIAL ACCEPTANCE

Even when all other factors for having an additional child are in place, there is one area that might still hold a couple back: social acceptance.

---

17    *Sefer Hachinuch* 166:6. See *Niddah* 31b.
18    *Koheles* 2:13.
19    *Koheles* 8:1.

Social pressure might be subtle, but it can be immensely powerful. It may be just a matter-of-fact comment highlighting tight financial ability, the lack of flexibility, the look and orderliness in the home, or other similar areas of sensitivity. At times, it may just be an unspoken smirk or look that says it all. These comments may not only come from strangers, but often from loving and even well-meaning friends and family. Sometimes, it can merely be the norms and expectations of the local society that places tremendous pressure on a family that chooses to live differently.

Generally speaking, there are two forms of behavior:

- The first is dictated by the rational and sensible self of the person. In this case, the person is prepared to change their conduct considering education and understanding.
- The second is when reason dictates one form of conduct but is too weak to prevail in the face of the emotional backlash. This occurs because the person, as our Sages put it, "is in the possession of their hearts," where the emotional side of the person is more powerful than their mind.[20]

"Falling into the possession of the heart" often occurs when a person's principles become subject to ridicule or mockery by their peers. In such instances, the person is prone to succumb to social pressure even when they are fully aware of their misconduct.

In Judaism, there is much attention given to this form of challenge. The Code of Jewish Law chooses to include this idea in its very first paragraph: "Be bold as a leopard—not to be ashamed of those who mock him in his service of G-d."[21]

The rational side of a person is quite limited. The most powerful elements in the human being exist in the suprarational. The suprarational can elevate the person to a level greater and higher than the rational, or it can lower the person to a level much lower than the rational can ever take him to. To overcome suprarational evil, a Jew must employ the tenacity and resolve of supra-rational good.

---

20   *Bereishis Rabbah* 34:10.
21   *Tur* and *Shulchan Aruch, Orach Chaim* 1:1.

The mechanics of overcoming social pressure in matters of Divine service are laid out in our sources in several different ways. Two of the primary ones are as follows:

- The injunction in the Code of Jewish Law (*Shulchan Aruch*) not to be ashamed of those who ridicule is prefaced by a quote from *Tehillim*:[22] "I have set G-d before me always." The *Shulchan Aruch* explains how the conduct of a person is radically different when they are in the presence of a king than when they are in private. The conduct of a Jew must always be in cognizance of the fact that G-d is "standing above him and watching his actions." The realization that G-d Himself is watching at this very moment, waiting in anticipation that the person should make the right decision—this itself can propel the individual to do what is right against all odds.

- The Torah refers to the Jewish people as "*am kesheh oref*—a stiff-necked nation."[23] Although the Torah describes this as a negative trait, our Sages tell us that it can actually be harnessed for greatness. As elaborated upon above, every Jew by virtue of their G-dly soul, possesses the capability of remaining unfazed and unwavering in the face of spiritual challenge. It is this resilience that allowed Jews of all times to withstand every conceivable form of torture and degradation and to stand firm in their covenant with G-d and their commitment to Him. When all else fails, it is this kind of resolve that a Jew can always fall back on. *Mesiras nefesh*—the impossibility for a Jew to tear himself away from G-d—is at the core of every Jewish man and woman. It can be employed in any given time or situation.

Having said all this, there is an additional dimension that takes this subject a step further:

---

22    16:8.

23    *Devarim* 34:9; see *Shemos Rabbah* 42.

Social pressure and expectation assume that the person in question measures themselves against the same standards as their peers. When the two parties are of entirely different nature, there can be little room for comparison in the first place. In such a case, the "pressure" emanating from the expectations of such surroundings is basically a non-issue.

An ambassador to a foreign country need not feel pressure of integrating into the life and culture of his country of residence. Although he lives and works in a different country, he is not a citizen like all the rest. On the contrary, his entire presence is to represent his home country to others.

By the same token, a Jew cannot measure his own lifestyle by the standards of the non-Jewish world. A Jew is different. A Jew is an ambassador.

As mentioned previously, the Torah terms the Jewish people an "*am kadosh*—a holy people." We are enjoined to live in a "holy" way.[24] The concept of holiness is that a particular item is different and apart from the rest. It carries something of G-dly nature.

Being a Jew is to be holy. To be a Jew is to be counted among those who possess a G-dly soul and are charged with the mission of bringing holiness to the world. A Jew must see himself as being *put into* the world—not a part of it. "A prisoner cannot release himself from prison."[25] Being a part of the world, even if a very important part, inevitably means the inability of elevating it, for that which needs elevation, cannot elevate. To elevate the world, the Jew needs to be—and consistently remain—above it.

Being a Jew cannot be viewed merely as an *element* in one's life; rather it defines one's life. The mitzvos relate to every detail of a Jew's life because the very definition of life for a Jew is different; it is defined by a holy cause.

As with all other areas in life, the Jew has a unique mission with regard to childbearing. With each additional child, a Jewish couple fulfills their G-dly purpose in a way that cannot be rivaled. In our day and age,

---

24   See *Shemos* 19:6. *Vayikra* 19:2.
25   See *Berachos* 5b.

fulfilling this mitzvah creates a radically different lifestyle for the Jew than for those in the non-Jewish world. But this will only be a cause of social pressure to the Jew if their idea of life is that it is essentially meant to be similar to everyone else. The truth, however, cannot be further from this. A Jew is different. A Jew could only feel disadvantaged or deprived if he lacks the internalization of his crucial and unique role in this world.

Upon their Exodus from Egypt, the Jewish people were given the title "*Tzivos Hashem*—the Army of G-d." Every detail in the life of a soldier is radically different than that of his civilian counterpart. A soldier can never measure his successes or failures by the same standards as a civilian. His mission—indeed his very life—has an entirely different nature and meaning. Furthermore, being part of the army puts the soldier in a special and unique league. It is something that he should hold with tremendous distinction; it should make him deeply proud.

By the same token, being a part of the Jewish people must fill the Jew with humility and awe, but, simultaneously, with genuine dignity and pride. "*Geon Yaakov*—the pride of Yaakov" is an expression of the deep distinction in which Jews throughout the ages carried their unique privilege and intense responsibility.

The Jewish people are likened to "children of kings."[26] A prince and princess represent the monarchy and must therefore lead distinct and highly meticulous lives. This, however, is only due to the great privilege and immense distinction of being born a child of royalty.

In closing, the obvious antidote to unwanted social pressure lies in fulfilling the duty our Sages give us: "Assume for yourself a teacher and acquire for yourself a friend."[27] As Jews, we are obligated to surround ourselves as much as possible with good influence and inspiration.[28] The more demanding a task, the more support and inspiration is necessary.

---

26    See *Bava Metzia* 113b.

27    *Mishnah Avos* 1:6.

28    See *Rambam, Hilchos Deos*, chap. 6.

## FINAL THOUGHTS

Our discussion in this part of the book has addressed various practical concerns and the Torah approach attached to them. These have been examined on a conceptual level, describing what the general approach to these issues should be.

It remains obvious, though, that each family situation is unique, and many factors shape the distinct challenges of each individual. Like any other mitzvah, the concept behind it can be explained, the challenges associated with it can be generally addressed, but then must come the work of the individual with their own situation on the ground level.

As emphasized in the introduction to this part of the book, the success of properly raising children in larger families has been achieved countless times. A wide array of books, articles, blogs, discussion forums, and social media groups are available on the subject at the click of a button. The most valuable wisdom can assuredly be found with older parents of large Jewish families who have decades of experience behind them.

> If someone says, "I have worked hard, but I have not been successful," do not believe him. If someone says, "I have not worked hard, and I have been successful," do not believe him. If someone says, "I have worked hard, and I have been successful," believe him! (*Megillah* 6b)

PART 4

# Birth Spacing

# CHAPTER 12

# Space or Delay

## REEXAMINING MOTIVATION

A major element in the discussion about having additional children is the question of frequency of birth, or, as it has become known, birth spacing. Many of the concerns mentioned above not only pertain to couples deciding whether to have another child at all, but also to those who have made the theoretical decision in the affirmative but are considering delaying the next child to a later time.

It is important to note that our discussion here is outside the realm of when there is an actual necessity for such a practice. Our discussion is rather directed at the prolonging of time between children *beyond* what may be necessary for a Torah validated reason. (These will be discussed later in chapter 13.)

By way of repetition, we must once again emphasize what has already been discussed above at length. The Torah's position is that an additional Jewish child is *infinitely necessary* and *an incredible blessing*. Therefore, as a rule, a Jewish couple should endeavor to have additional children without unreasonably putting off or delaying this immense privilege and sacred task. In general, the Torah encourages us never to put off or delay a mitzvah.[1] The mitzvah of having additional children is no different.

Depending on the situation, there will be variations as to the outright halachic obligation of having another child without excess delay. At times it is a clear obligation, at other times less so. Nevertheless, when the question of spacing comes up, it is crucial that parents ask themselves some honest questions: What is my true motivation? Why do I feel this way? The desire for a prolonged space between births may need to be altogether reexamined.

After the concerns have been addressed, we can turn to the many aspects of deep pleasure and tremendous joy that accompany the addition of every child (see part 2). For both parents—especially the mother—these are rewarding experiences that are unmatched by any other. All things considered, prolonging the time between births will deprive both parents and the rest of the family of a more imminent arrival of the greatest of gifts.

## A BLESSING IN ITS TIME

Aside for all we have discussed until now, there are some additional points which are particularly relevant to the spacing issue:

The Torah contains many blessings given to the Jewish people if they heed the Divine commandments. One of these blessings reads: "I will grant your rains in their season."[2] The blessing here is not only the rain itself but that G-d will give it at the best time possible.[3] This idea applies not only to rain, but to every blessing whose timing is of significance.

The reality of childbirth is that every part of it—from conception to pregnancy and successful delivery—is entirely in the hands of G-d and is directly orchestrated by Him. The human being may have the ability, to some degree, to *withhold* having more children, but insofar as *having* a healthy child with all the complexity it entails, this depends entirely on the blessing from Above.

---

1    See *Mechilta, Parshas Bo* 9.
2    *Vayikra* 26:4.
3    See *Rashi* ad loc.

After achieving forgiveness for the sin of the Golden Calf, the Torah relates how Moshe made a bold request of G-d: "Show me your glory," he asked. This request is understood by the commentaries as Moshe's desire to grasp and perceive G-d Himself. But Moshe's request was turned down. "You will not be able to see My face, for no human can see My face and live."[4]

In this regard, the Talmud makes an incredible statement. It tells us that there was actually a time when "seeing the face of G-d" was available to Moshe, but he himself had turned down the opportunity. The reference here is to Moshe's first encounter with G-d that took place at the burning bush. After introducing Himself to Moshe as the G-d of his forefathers, the verse tells us that Moshe "hid his face, for he was afraid to gaze toward G-d."[5]

This, says the Talmud, was a lost opportunity. "When I wanted [to show you My glory] you did not want, now that you want, I do not want."[6] According to this Talmudic passage, human beings are not inherently unable to see "G-d's face"; rather, it is G-d's decision whether to show it to man or not.[7]

The idea behind this is obviously far from being some kind of offense on G-d's part to Moshe's initial decline of G-dly closeness. It is rather, as every part of Torah, a timeless lesson. In this case, it is a lesson in the dynamics of a Divine blessing. Similar to rain, there is tremendous significance in the timing of any Heavenly gift.

The various calculations we make about our position in life are finite and limited. G-d, on the other hand, sees all and knows all. G-d possesses the ability not only of the blessing itself, but of giving it at the appropriate time. In fact, as this piece of Talmud indicates, if a person fails to accept G-d's gift at the time He deems appropriate, there are no guarantees that a similar opportunity will present itself at a later time.

---

4   *Shemos* 33:18-20.
5   Ibid 3:6.
6   *Berachos* 7a.
7   See *Maharsha* to *Berachos* ibid.

Any time that G-d wills a child to be conceived and born is a great blessing. The choice that a couple has is whether to allow this blessing to be bestowed in the time that G-d deems it to be best, or to "step in" and decide for themselves when the appropriate time might be.

The unknowns of life, both of the parents and of the potential child, are vast. There is no firmer foundation for life than allowing the Creator Himself to decide the ideal time for its commencement. In this way, a couple can rest assured that the timing of having their child is as perfect as possible.

It must be emphasized, as mentioned in the beginning of this discussion, that sometimes the will of G-d and the "right time" for the birth of another child will indeed be at a later time. This is the case when a halachic ruling to this end is determined by a qualified rabbi in the field. The details of this will be discussed in the next chapter.

# CHAPTER 13

# The Exceptions

## "AN EXCESS OF GOOD"

The Talmud relates the following story:

> There was once a severe drought in the Land of Israel. At this time, there lived a great Sage and tzaddik by the name of Choni Hame'agel. The people sent a message to Choni asking him to pray that rain should fall. Choni prayed, but no rain fell.
>
> Seeing this, he drew a circle in the dust, stood inside it, and said before G-d, "Master of the Universe! Your children have turned their faces toward me, as I am like a member of Your household. Therefore, I take an oath by Your great name that I will not move from here until you have mercy upon Your children and answer their prayers for rain."
>
> Rain began to trickle down, but only in small droplets. His students said to him, "Rabbi, we have seen that you can perform great wonders, but this quantity of rain is not enough to ensure that we will not die. It appears to us that a small amount of

129

rain is falling only to enable you to absolve you of your oath, but it is not nearly enough to save us."

Choni said to G-d, "I did not ask for this, but [rather] for rain to fill the cisterns, ditches, and caves!" Rain began to fall furiously; each drop was as big as the mouth of a barrel, and the Sages estimated that no drop was less than a "log" in size.[1] His students said to him: "Rabbi, we have seen that you can call on G-d to perform miracles, and we will not die, but now it appears to us that rain is falling only to destroy the world!"

Choni again said before G-d, "I did not ask for this harmful rain either, but for rain of benevolence, blessing, and generosity." Subsequently, the rains fell in their standard manner, until all the people sought higher ground and ascended to the Temple Mount due to the rain. They said to him, "Rabbi, just as you prayed that the rains should fall, so too, pray that they should stop."

Choni said to them, "This is the tradition that I received: one does not pray over an excess of good. Nevertheless, bring me a bull. I will sacrifice it as a thanks-offering and pray at the same time." They brought him a bull for a thanks-offering. He placed his two hands on its head and said before G-d, "Master of the Universe, Your nation Israel, whom You brought out of Egypt, cannot bear either an excess of good or an excess of punishment. You grew angry with them and withheld rain, and they were unable to bear it. You bestowed upon them too much good, and they were also unable to bear it. May it be Your will that the rain stops and that there be relief to the world."

Immediately, the wind blew, the clouds dispersed, the sun shone, and everyone went out to the fields and gathered for themselves truffles and mushrooms that had sprouted in the heavy rain.[2]

---

1   A measurement equivalent to six eggs.
2   *Taanis* 23a.

Some parallels can be made from this Talmudic story to our subject matter. Rain is both a necessity and a blessing. But like rain, sometimes there is a true difficulty on the part of the recipient in accepting an abundance of blessing. A situation may arise when a couple feels that having another child is a situation of "You bestowed upon them too much good, and they were unable to bear it." Like in this story, this inability may be entirely beyond the control of the couple in question.

The following are some of the instances when, after personal (and/ or professional) analysis, a rabbi who specializes in this area should be consulted:

- The youngest child is still very young, particularly if they are nursing.
- There exists a lack of physical, mental, or emotional strength on the part of either parent, particularly the mother.
- There exists a history of frequent or ongoing cases of miscarriage.
- Either parent possesses a fragile or low-tolerance personality.
- Existing children have significant physical, psychological, or spiritual challenges.
- There is tension in the marriage.
- The family is experiencing severe financial pressure.
- There is evident or looming failure in familial or financial management.

The necessity in involving a rabbi in this decision is twofold:

- First, the question involves several major aspects in Jewish law, much of which is not commonly studied.
- Second, the various factors involved in the question must be weighed carefully and put into a Torah perspective. Only then can a correct analysis of the situation be determined.

It is incumbent on a couple to be upfront and honest about their situation so that a proper conclusion may be reached. Aside from the knowledge of the halachah regarding this matter, it is also a holy obligation of a rabbi to be highly sensitive both to the imperative of having an additional child *and* to the current family dynamic. In addition, the responsibility of a rabbi is not to merely be a source of information, but also to be a source of inspiration and encouragement in following the Torah way.

After deliberation, the conclusion by the rabbi may be that the couple should put childbearing on hold for the time being (or even indefinitely).

A situation like this may be compared to other situations we often find in Jewish life. For example, when a person is sick, and a halachic ruling has been issued forbidding him to fast on Yom Kippur. We know of several instances that when finding themselves is such a situation, rabbis and pious Jews composed heartfelt prayers expressing their feelings about having to do something that under normal circumstances was unthinkable. Yet, they understood that in this situation, the will of the Almighty was that they eat and not fast. Doing so was therefore a mitzvah, and like all mitzvos, this too was to be done with joy.

But the litmus test for spiritual maturity comes at the time when the situation of danger passes. Using the Yom Kippur analogy, although fasting is painful and definitely more difficult than eating, the serious Jew will give thanks to G-d and be tremendously grateful for the ability of once again fulfilling a mitzvah he was deprived of previously.

The parallel to our subject matter is self-understood.

# 𝒜 Jewish 𝒜pproach for the 𝒩on-Jew

## A MENTALITY

The material in this work has focused on the Jewish approach to family planning. As such, it is a book primarily directed to the Jewish community. Still, the Torah contains not only instruction for Jews, but is also a guide for humanity at large. In addition, the Torah obligates a Jew to actively promote the Torah's universal values to the members of the wider, non-Jewish community.[1]

The Torah's system for the world at large falls into two distinct categories:

- The first are laws which are strictly binding. These, for the most part, are shared by Jew and non-Jew alike. They are the laws of social justice and civil order that make up the fabric of a good and moral society.
- The second is classified not as laws but as "general imperatives."

---

1   See *Rambam, Hilchos Melachim* 8:13; *Tosfos Yom Tov Avos* 3:14.

These are principles that are often put as obligations on the Jew, and by extension create the desired standard for humanity at large.

One of the areas that answers to the second category is childbirth. In the final analysis, it seems that although childbearing is an obligation on the Jew, it is not a technical obligation on a non-Jew. What is in place, however, is a general imperative for the non-Jew to marry and procreate. This is expressed using the words of the prophet: "He [G-d] did not create it [the world] for emptiness; He fashioned it to be inhabited."[2]

As a program and way of life, a non-Jew must know that the will of G-d is for him or her to find a suitable spouse, marry, and have children.[3] This program, as it were, is stated by the Torah as part of the creation narrative with regard to Adam and Chavah: "Therefore, a man shall leave his father and his mother, and cleave to his wife, and they shall become one flesh."[4] The idea of becoming "one flesh" refers to the bearing of a child, in whom the parents' flesh becomes one.[5]

Each human being has a unique role in this world. This function can only be fulfilled when the human soul is brought down to earth within a human body. Each life on earth is therefore indispensable.

Moreover, the Torah emphasizes that every human being is created "in the image of G-d."[6] However this is understood, the idea is that each individual person has an element of G-dliness in the very fabric of their being. This is why human life is sacred and non-negotiable.

Facilitating another human life is the affirmation of the ultimate necessity in every individual. Regardless of how many children are already born to a family, having another child is a gift from G-d and a tremendous privilege. For the parents, it is the ability to once again partner with G-d in the project of another human being. In a word—another child is a blessing.

---

2   *Yeshayahu* 45:18.
3   See *Aruch Hashulchan, Even Haezer* 1:5.
4   *Bereishis* 2:24.
5   *Rashi* ad loc.
6   *Bereishis* 1:26-7.

Furthermore, the parents of a yet unconceived child must realize that there is a moral question at stake: Is it correct that the decision regarding a life on earth be entirely up to the whim of two other mortals? Can the very life of a human boil down to the question of whether or not a couple feels like having it? Taking such an approach to *actual* life would be horrifying to any moral person. But what about potential life? Can the attitude toward the potential be so dramatically different? The question is not only with regard to the life of one child, but to its children and grandchildren till the end of time.

In contrast, the strong overtones of a secular culture encourage people, especially women, not to see themselves as subjected or compelled to have children. They should rather live by choice and be free to choose the lifestyle they desire without the "interference" of multiple children.

Regardless of the possibly good intentions by many in previous centuries, it can now be said for certain that as a result of the rhetoric associated with "family planning," the project of having children has been severely decentralized and de-sanctified in the minds of an entire generation. It has led to the notion of being "tied down" or "suffocated" by the fate of parenthood and particularly motherhood. In worst case scenarios, it has led to countless cases of misery and betrayal.

The dominant trend has also led to mass consumption of oral contraceptives, a medium which all agree is, at the very least, unhealthy. To date, "the pill" still remains a primary form of contraception, even in view of its hazards.[7]

Moreover, a frequent outcome of the mindset associated with family planning is the abortion of an unwanted child. As a rule, abortion is forbidden by Torah and is considered murder.[8] In 2014, approximately nineteen percent of all pregnancies in the US (excluding spontaneous miscarriages) ended in abortion.[9] The percentage is higher in many

---

7    Tara Haelle, "Pill Remains Most Common Birth Control Method," Webmd, December 11, 2014, https://www.webmd.com/sex/birth-control/news/20141211/the-pill-remains-most-common-method-of-birth-control-us-report-shows#1.

8    See *Sanhedrin* 57a; *Rambam, Hilchos Melachim* 9:4.

9    Abort73.com, "U.S. Abortion Statistics," Loxafamosity Ministries, last updated on February 19, 2019, https://abort73.com/abortion_facts/us_abortion_statistics/.

other developed countries. Even when the parents (often it is only the mother) choose not to kill the fetus, there can obviously remain much to be desired in the upbringing of a child who at the very onset was "unwanted."

From a Torah perspective, it is imperative that this damaging mentality regarding childbirth be rectified. Governments and enterprises would do much better in promoting and glorifying the nuclear family, rather than endorsing the mentality of "choice" that has been so instrumental in the destruction of the family. On every count, people would be healthier and happier in the long term.

This is not to say that young people should marry and have children without any plan of sustainability. In Judaism, this is referred to as "the way of the fools."[10] The idea here is that having children should be seen as a privilege and joy, a sacred endeavor, and the highest vocation for the mother.

There may indeed be times when contraception is necessary. This "necessity," however, must be put into correct context; namely, that while another child is a tremendous gift and a sacred responsibility, a couple may have a genuine and honest need to withhold themselves from this. In this case, contraception can be used for the purpose of maintaining an intimate life between husband and wife. (As should be understood, this approach precludes intimacy—with or without contraceptive—outside of wedlock, an action that the Torah prohibits to Jews, and at least frowns upon regarding non-Jews.)

In addition, it may also be worthy to address another common form of "planning"—the delay of having children in the quest to first be fully established financially. This desire, in its elementary sense, is praiseworthy; but it also has its boundaries and proportions. This is chiefly because having a family is fundamental to the mission of the human being on earth, and therefore fundamental to human fulfillment and happiness. It must therefore be viewed as at least equal to any other essential element of adulthood.

---

10    *Rambam, Hilchos Deos* 5:11.

No child was ever self-sufficient enough to raise and educate themselves on their own. Every milestone of youth is achieved with the help of parents and family. By the same token, marrying and starting a family is an integral achievement of young adult life. Thus, it can and should be brought about through a joint effort of parents and family.

## SUSTAINABILITY AND THE ENVIRONMENT

In recent times, the global population has risen dramatically. Whereas two hundred years ago there were less than one billion people on earth, today's estimates run well over the seven billion mark. Since all agree that there is a finite number of people that nature can properly sustain, many voice concerns as to the overall encouragement of childbirth on a global level.

There are several points here to be made. The question of continuing childbirth in view of population increase must be viewed as a question from an individual family. Although global population is on the rise, the picture on the ground in certain countries is a lot more complicated.

In many developed countries, there is a serious "birth dearth" where people are having far fewer children than the replacement level. In 2016, the number of births in every major English-speaking country was less than 2.1 per woman—the figure given for replacement level.[11] Russia, China, Brazil, Japan, and basically all European countries are in the same category. In these places, having another child serves the collective good in a very real way.

Regardless of the statistics, there is one thing that must remain clear: Every life is sacred, necessary, and non-negotiable. The chance, possibility, and ability to bring another life to this world is supreme. The implication of this is that any and every measure must be exhausted—collectively and individually—in order that another life on earth be sustained. Natural and human resources are there to serve life—not the other way around. Cultures whose principles allow precedence for other concerns over the birth of a child inevitably promote

---

11    https://data.worldbank.org/indicator/SP.DYN.TFRT.IN.

the idea that human life is in fact negotiable, unnecessary, and certainly not sacred. The countless cases of abortion in these cultures confirms this fact. As mentioned, the Torah's position on unwarranted abortion is that it is a flagrant violation of human life, and generally speaking has the legal status of murder.

In China, for example, when state limitations on childbirth were enforced, women by the millions were coerced to abort or be sterilized if they were found pregnant with an additional child. Little else can match the violation of basic dignity and respect for human life than the application of such a policy.

It is hypothetically conceivable that an increase in population could become problematic to the point where limiting population growth is the *only* alternative to otherwise severe consequences. (It is worth noting that a provision for such a situation may have been made by the Torah not making childbirth an absolute obligation for humanity at large.) In such an instance, the implementation of any population control, whether for the individual or for the collective population, must be done with the utmost of caution. It must be viewed as an emergency and abnormal situation which must be terminated as soon as the opportunity presents itself. No person or entity may ever place itself as an "accomplice to sin"—in this case, the cardinal sin of murder and a host of other moral crimes against the mother. Many forms of contraception are also problematic in this regard.[12]

All in all, the human being is charged with the sacred responsibility of upholding the sanctity of human life, mandated to him directly by the Creator of life Himself.

---

12   There are many forms of surgical interventions which according to many are forbidden both to Jew and non-Jew. For an overview of these, see Encyclopedia Halachtit-Refuit, Sirrus.

THIS BOOK HAS BEEN MADE POSSIBLE
WITH THE GENEROUS ASSISTANCE OF

# Ben Terner

# Rabbi Moshe and Etti Drizin

WITH HEARTFELT BLESSING FOR CONTINUED
SUCCESS IN ALL YOUR ENDEAVORS

# About the Author

MENDEL DUBOV serves as rabbi and director of Chabad in Sussex County, NJ, and is a faculty member at the Rabbinical College of America. He has previously published several books on Jewish thought and is an ongoing contributor to Chabad.org, one of the largest Jewish websites.

# About Mosaica Press

MOSAICA PRESS is an independent publisher of Jewish books. Our authors include some of the most profound, interesting, and entertaining thinkers and writers in the Jewish community today. Our books are available around the world. Please visit us at www.mosaicapress.com or contact us at info@mosaicapress.com. We will be glad to hear from you.